"Thank you all from the pit of my burning, nauseous stomach for your letters and concerns during the last years."

—Kurt Cobain
April, 1994

NEVER FADE AWAY

THE KURT COBAIN STORY

DAVE THOMPSON

St. Martin's Paperbacks

NEVER FADE AWAY: THE KURT COBAIN STORY

Copyright © 1994 by Dave Thompson.

Front cover photograph copyright © Frank Micoletta/Outline. Back cover photograph courtesy AP/Wide World Photos.

ISBN: 0-312-95463-8
EAN: 80312-95463-5

Printed in the United States of America

St. Martin's Paperbacks edition / June 1994

20 19 18 17 16 15 14 13 12 11 10

1

The first reports were vague, a dull rumor which percolated out into post-rush hour Seattle traffic. The body of a young man, an apparent suicide, had just been discovered in the Seattle home of Kurt Cobain.

The cause of death seemed to have been a shotgun blast to the head; initial reports suggested that the body had lain there for at least a day before it was discovered by a visiting electrician; and there was the distinct possibility that the body, clad in jeans, a long-sleeved shirt and black sneakers, was Cobain's. That, in a nutshell, was what the city had to go on.

But in many ways, it was enough. The body was discovered at 8:40 A.M.; fifty minutes later, local radio station KXRX was broadcasting the news. By 10 A.M., it seemed as though every phone in the city was ringing, as disbelieving fans called their friends to check their ears. Have you heard? Is it true? What else do you know? Then, once it was certain that nobody knew more than anyone else, people fell back on the radio and their wits. It was going to be a very long day.

The drama which shattered Seattle out of its early morning stupor formally hit the headlines on April 8th, 1994. But in painful actuality, it had been unfolding a month by then, ever since Kurt Cobain ingested a theoretically lethal combination of champagne and the drug Riapnol, then collapsed on an Italian hotel room floor.

For a few moments then, too, a good proportion of the western world held its breath, and by the time CNN announced, erroneously of course, that the singer had died, people were already expecting the worst.

The first statements from Nirvana's management, Gold Mountain, were frustratingly vague. The *Seattle Times* simply quoted Gold Mountain spokeswoman Janet Billig's explanation that Kurt had been prescribed pain killers after Nirvana's recently completed European tour, for the stomach pains which had plagued him most of his life. A combination of these drugs and alcohol then produced what she called "complications".

A more thorough, if still incomplete, explanation was released later in the day: "Kurt Cobain slipped into a coma at 6 A.M. European Standard Time. . . . The coma was induced by a combination of the flu and fatigue, on top of prescription painkillers and champagne. While Cobain has not awoken, he shows significant signs, said his doctors." Billig later added, "the vital signs came back, and he's opened his eyes. I don't know if he's talking lucidly, but he's moving his hands. His wife—singer Courtney Love—and daughter [18-month-old Frances Bean] are with him."

Still, there were gaps in the story, gaps which a number of reporters felt might be filled in Seattle. An "insider [at *People*] contacted *The Rocket*, the city's own private music paper, and informed them that 'editors were already marking off the turf: "if he dies, it's the cover, if he remains in a coma it's three pages, if he's up and walking soon, it's half a page." ' "

Kurt was still unconscious when the conversation took place—it's "nice", the *Rocket*'s Johnny Renton deadpanned, "to know how the press sets its standards of integrity, isn't it?"

But that sense of cynicism affected a lot of people, this time, as well. Another false alarm; we've heard it all before.

Because Cobain was known to have had a heroin problem, reporters and fans from around the world assumed a heroin overdose was being covered up, rather than investigating what turned out to have been a suicide attempt.

Later it was clear that Rome really had been just a reprieve—and an unintentional reprieve at that. Kurt had meant to kill himself on that occasion, too, as the note he reportedly left for Courtney proved.

Returning home to Seattle from his Italian misadventure, Kurt lost very little time in finding his way back into the city's narcotic underbelly. It is not, after all, as though he had far to look.

Heroin in Seattle, says Courtney, is "like apples in the orchard. It's falling off the . . . trees." Amazed by the ease with which the drug could be purchased around the city, she continued, "The Seattle police won't do anything about it. I asked them, 'don't you get embarrassed when you (hear) that Seattle is famous for grunge, cappuccino and heroin?' "

Chris Novoselic, Nirvana's six foot seven inch bass player, was quick to hit back—Kurt had been Courtney's husband, but he had been his friend as well, and he was convinced that the drug was only part of the story, and an insignificant fraction at that.

"Just blaming [Kurt's death] on smack is stupid. People have been taking smack for a hundred years. You can get [it] in any town. [And] smack was just a small part of his life." No, he did not have any answers yet . . . but neither did anybody else.

Or maybe they did. Seattle might once have been voted America's most liveable city, but in the popular mind, it's also the most die-able. Two of America's most notorious serial murderers, Ted Bundy and the Green

River Killer, operated in the immediate vicinity, but even before them, Seattle was known for its darkness, a dense spiritual darkness which enveloped all that it touched. Was it mere coincidence that when director David Lynch conceived the cult TV series *Twin Peaks*, it was the Northwest in which he chose to house its demented denizens?

Or that when the rock'n'roll tourist arrives in town for the first time, it's Death, not Life, which will haunt his itinerary. It matters not that the city has a tenacious grip on America's rock'n'roll sensibilities. Seattle has little to show for its efforts, nevertheless.

True, there is the Sub Pop shop, a few doors down from the Moore Theater, where you can purchase souvenirs of the label that shaped a nation's taste and sold a million boots for Doc Martin; and the Edgewater Inn, where Led Zeppelin allegedly entertained a redhead with a sand shark; and Sand Point Way, where sculptor Doug Hollis' Sound Garden stands howling to the winds.

But there is no Whiskey a-Go-Go, with three decades of history; no CBGBs, the birthplace of Punk; no Route 66 or 128. In other words, while Seattle bristles with rock'n'roll footnotes, there are very few firm chapter headings. What it does have are final paragraphs.

In Renton, to the south of the city limits, Greenwood Memorial Park houses the mortal remains of Jimi Hendrix, the guitarist who changed the face of modern rock'n'roll. On First Avenue, downtown, a wall outside the Vogue has been given over to graffiti and the soul of Andrew Wood, the voice of Mother Love Bone.

Stefanie Sargent, guitarist with 7 Year Bitch, died in Seattle in 1992; so did the Gits' Mia Zapata, savagely murdered just twelve short months later. The darkness which inspired *Twin Peaks*, which so permeates the Pacific Northwest that even local residents, who should be used to it, have reluctlantly adopted the phrase "Northwest noir"; that darkness has a special attraction for rock'n'roll, and though those deaths are totally unconnected, they are united in the psyche of the city.

And now there's another site to add to the tour books, set back from the street and shrouded in greenery, a low wall topped by impenetrable bushes, isolated in the way that only a million-dollar home can be. 171 Lake Washington Boulevard, which the Cobains bought four months earlier, and where he ended his life.

Kurt made no secret about his use of drugs, although friends insisted that he was off them as often as on, and even smack was medicinal, rather than fun. In his battle against those chronic stomach agonies, heroin was the only drug he knew of which not only alleviated the physical pain, but also blotted out the mental anguish he suffered.

Over the years, the term "reluctant superstar" has been so overdone, that today, it's all but meaningless. All one needs to do, it seems, is curse out a few photographers, then turn up late for an interview, and suddenly it's being splashed everywhere. It's become particularly popular in the last decade or so, all the more so because show-business has been desperately trying to demystify itself for just as long.

"Stars" are no longer untouchable deities, abseiling down the face of Mount Olympus to bestow their blessings on a meek and servile public. These days, they're folk just like you and me, with problems and toothaches like us, and the superstar excesses which we once endured, the drink and drugs and the multiple marriages, are not excesses any longer. These days, they're weaknesses, and instead of swooning at our idols' feet, today we're expected to pat them on the head. Like, "it must be *so* tough for you, and I should be so unlucky," because really, idols should not be demystified; they should be left in sacred sanctuaries to sparkle and to shine.

Tabloid sales might disagree, but the psychology behind them sure doesn't. People *need* celebrities who they can look up to, and though they voraciously devour their problems, it's *because* they're celebrities, that those problems matter. Dust the stardust from the superstars and what have you got? Mrs. Higgins down the road, complaining of her bunions; Mr. Potter at the bus stop, groaning when it rains. Remember when your parents would say, as you played the latest Sex Pistols record, "They don't write them like they used to do?" Give it another couple of years, then look at the bands who your kids are listening to. "They don't *make* them like they used to do, either."

Kurt Cobain certainly wasn't "made like they used to" be made, although on paper, he had all the hallmarks. In the brief three years since Nirvana exploded out of nowhere (in the wider sense, nowhere, although they'd already been together for five years by then), Cobain has been compared to most, if not all, of Rock's greatest stars.

John Lennon? Who else wrote such achingly personal songs?

Elvis Presley? Who else had so electrifying an effect on an apparently moribund market?

Johnny Rotten? Ditto, but with an extra, in-built, marketable cuddliness. You might impale yourself on those piercing blue eyes, but when you got up close, and listened to that low, warm, voice, one moment so serious, the next, breaking out with an infectious half-giggle, it was impossible to walk away from Kurt Cobain not believing that you'd just met your very best friend. So what if the next time, he ignored you? That first time was yours, and no one could take it away from you.

Then, when the news came of his death, it hit you even harder, because you'd never be able to repeat that moment, not even in your own mind, because even your dreams are haunted by the details the tabloids forgot to put in, like the mess that the shotgun must have made of his head, and the state of his mind as he did it. A reluctant superstar? At times, Kurt Cobain was a reluctant human being. His fame was simply the arsenic-tainted icing on a very rotten cake.

In the note he left alongside his body, Kurt confessed "I haven't felt the excitement of . . . creating music along with really writing something for so many years now." His enthusiasm came in spurts—the week before Nirvana played their first show in three months at the 1992 New Music Seminar in New York, Kurt could scarcely control his excitement at the prospect of putting together a short acoustic set. He'd got the songs, and they weren't all screaming Punk Rock. "I think people will be surprised."

Instead, they were horrified. Four songs tacked to the end of a blistering show in a sweat-drenched Roseland, and the crowd was booing like it was Dylan at Newport. "Play some rock'n'roll!" Later mobs were more restrained, and by the time Nirvana treated MTV to an hour of the stuff, people were actually suggesting that the next Nirvana album should follow the pattern unerringly. But by then, maybe, Kurt had already lost interest. He was a rock'n'roller now. Would he ever be allowed to become something else? Not in this lifetime.

Hopelessly adrift within the demands of his own career, Kurt was reaching out, but no one could quite grasp him. In early March, as he prepared for the final concerts of his life, Kurt telephoned his cousin, Art Cobain, from Germany. No real reason, just to chat. But there was one thing he said which stuck with Art. "He said he was getting really fed up with his way of life," Art told *People* magazine. And that phrase again, "he really seemed to be reaching out." Unfortunately, the only solace Art could give, was to invite Kurt to a forthcoming Cobain family reunion. He hadn't seen his cousin since childhood—he would never see him again.

Kurt's final words, the last things he would ever write

in his neat, but childlike scrawl, were addressed to his family, but aimed at the world.

"Sometimes I feel I should have a punch-in clock before I walk out on stage," Kurt wrote. He pleaded that he had done "everything in my power to appreciate it, . . . but it's not enough." Then Kurt confessed that he was "too sensitive," because he needed "to be slightly numb in order to regain the enthusiasm I once had as a child. . . ."

And the worst crime he could think of would be "to put people off by faking it, by pretending . . . I am having 100% fun."

To which his wife, Courtney Love, her voice shattered by emotion, but still intent on delivering his message to the thousands of fans gathered at a memorial service in Seattle, responded, "No Kurt, the worst crime I can think of is for you to just continue being a rock star when you fucking hate it. Just fucking stop!"

That was the message behind the meeting of friends, family and bandmates which Courtney convened within weeks of the couple's arrival back in Seattle, and just days after Kurt barricaded himself into a bathroom at the couple's Seattle home, threatening to kill himself, and this time, he'd get it right. He had a gun with him.

Courtney flew to the phone and called 911, but by the time the police arrived, the crisis had apparently already been averted. Kurt was still in the bathroom, but he was adamant that he wasn't suicidal—he was just hiding from his wife.

The police were convinced, after questioning Courtney, but they did not leave empty-handed—they also gathered up a .38 caliber Taurus revolver; a .380 Taurus handgun; a Beretta .380 semi-automatic handgun; and a Colt AR–15 semi-automatic rifle. Several of the guns had only just been returned to the Cobains following an altercation the previous summer—a remarkable arsenal for a man who had gone on record time and again expressing his dislike of firearms.

"I don't believe in them," he told *Alternative Press* in 1991, "but . . . I still think people have a right to own them." Journalist Susan Rees reported that "guns are mentioned in at least three songs [on *Nevermind*]."

That was Friday, March 18th; that weekend, Courtney and Nirvana bassist Chris Novoselic led the delegation of friends and family who intended confronting Kurt over his continued drug use—and delivering the simple message, shape up or ship out. As Tammi Blevins, a Gold Mountain spokeswoman, explained, "people close to him definitely did not want him on drugs."

Steve Chatoff, head of the Steps chemical dependency and mental health facility north of L.A., was intended to moderate the Intervention—if everything had gone according to plan, Chatoff would have returned to California with Kurt by his side. But it didn't. Someone reportedly warned Kurt what was going on, and that particular meeting was cancelled.

"There was no sense in my going after that," Chatoff told reporters. "You . . . need the element of surprise, to break through denial." And as another family friend told the *L.A. Times'* Robert Hilburn, "Kurt is so much in denial about a drug problem that it's unbelievable."

The Intervention went ahead regardless, a week later at Kurt and Courtney's home in Seattle's exclusive Madrona district. It was strictly informal, simply a gathering of the ten or so people who cared most about Kurt, who just wanted to sit down with him for a while and talk . . . Courtney and Chris; Danny Goldberg, now head of Atlantic Records; Pat Smear, the guitarist who had been working with Nirvana on and off since the previous fall; Dylan Carlson, one of Kurt's closest friends. . . .

"I told him, 'you've got to be a good daddy,' " Courtney said afterwards. " 'We've got to be good parents.' "

But Kurt wasn't interested. He would sit there for a while, quiet and seemingly acquiescent, his gaze passing from faces to his feet, but he didn't give a damn, not even when he heard that Gold Mountain had added their weight to the warning, reportedly by informing him that he would be dropped from their roster if he didn't clean up. Instead, he told Smear that they had work to do, and went down to the basement to rehearse a new song.

Courtney left Seattle on March 25th, and checked into the Peninsula Hotel in Beverley Hills, her base while she was in Los Angeles promoting her own band, Hole's, new album release, the now-ironically titled *Live Through This*.

The group had long since out-lived the once constant suggestions that Hole's own success was built around Courtney's husband, as opposed to her talent. Although they now shared both a record label (Geffen) and management company, Hole had consistently delivered the goods, first on 1991's *Pretty on the Inside*, on Caroline Records, which predates her relationship with Kurt, then touring with the Lemonheads to almost unbelievable acclaim, and finally serving up an album which, under almost any other circumstances, would have been instantly adjudged a classic.

As it was, it came close . . . like *Spin* magazine said when it profiled Love in the issue which had just hit the news stands when Kurt's death was announced, "junkie, star-fucker, gold-digger, Courtney Love took the blows, but through it all she did it her way. Now, with 1994's best album, Courtney has justified our love."

Even as she ironed out the last details of the release campaign, however; as she readied for the onslaught which inevitably awaited her in London, Hole's next port of call, Courtney's mind was elsewhere. She had left Kurt behind in Seattle, not out of choice, but out of necessity. He could be stubborn as a mule when his mind was set on something, and all she could hope to do, all anybody could ever do, was simply try to wear his resistance down. Now she was calling him every day, asking him to join her and maybe check out a rehab clinic she'd heard wonderful things about, the Exodus Recovery Center in Marina Del Rey.

Finally, Kurt gave in. He'd be down, he said, on March 28th, and he'd swing by the clinic and see what was happening. Courtney told a friend a few days later, "I was so proud of him."

The day before he left for L.A., Kurt apparently posted a lengthy message on the Internet computer network. It was mostly inconsequential ("so this is the Information Highway our illustrious VP has been jawing to the nation about?"), but did include a few tidbits about his plans for Nirvana's future—a "revamped" version of the last album's "Penny Royal Tea" which was planned for imminent release as a single; the "calmer, moodier" album they'd start work on in the fall.

"If you're expecting the same verse-chorus-verse . . . you have but two choices. Don't buy the new album . . . or get used to the fact that the band is changing. Longevity, folks."

He made only one reference to his recent personal crises, "I'm still a little freaked over the Rome thing, and need some time to rest and get over it. You'd think they could make a good milkshake, but no."

It wasn't only Kurt's health which concerned Courtney, however, even though that in itself would have been enough. The couple were still reeling from their 18-month-old encounter with the California child welfare authorities, swinging into action following a *Vanity Fair* article which claimed that Courtney maintained her *own* heroin habit while she was pregnant with her daughter, Frances Bean.

The crisis was averted, but it was still raised in conversation—even *Spin* brought it up when they'd talked earlier in the year.

"So, what about the actual charges?" writer Dennis Cooper asked.

"Innocent," Love replied. "Isn't that obvious?" Almost precisely one year before, on March 23rd, 1993, having spent the past three months submitting to regular urine tests and check-ups from social workers, the Cobains were informed that the authorities would be taking no further interest in Frances.

But as Courtney was well aware, it wasn't just her conduct during her pregnancy which had come under the microscope. It was her future behavior as well, and not only her's, but Kurt's too. Among the threats which she hurled at her husband as she begged him to check into rehab, was the knowledge of what could happen should his true state ever become public knowledge. "If we lose Frances. . . .

Once Kurt was in the Center, everyone breathed a huge sigh of relief. He was going to be okay. Two days later, Courtney's whole world came crashing down again.

The time Kurt Cobain spent in rehab remains undocumented—hardly surprisingly, of course. More than a week after he "jumped the fence" as Courtney put it, the Daniel Freeman Hospital, to which the Exodus center is affiliated, had still to confirm that he was even a patient.

But whatever happened, whatever treatment was meted out to Cobain, it doesn't seem to have made much difference. Kurt appeared to have vanished into thin air. Even Courtney was left in the dark. "I didn't know where he was. He never, ever disappeared like that. He always called me."

Instead, she was left with the memory of his last phone call, shortly before he vanished. "No matter what happens, I want you to know you made a really good record."

She asked him what he meant—what was likely to

happen? But he wouldn't say. "Just remember, no matter what happens, I love you."

On Sunday, April 3rd, according to a source close to the band, Courtney and Geffen arranged for private detectives to be hired, to trace Kurt. It was their belief that he would probably head back to Seattle.

Kurt was, in fact, already there. He arrived on Wednesday, March 30th, the same day he left the rehab facility, and contacted his old friend Dylan Carlson, guitarist with Olympia's band Earth, and the best man at Kurt and Courtney's marriage two years before. Kurt asked Dylan if he would go with him to buy a shotgun. "He said he wanted [it] for protection," Dylan explained later, which seemed reasonable enough.

So did Kurt's request that Dylan make the actual purchase. He was worried, Dylan said, that if he bought it in his own name, the police would simply come around and confiscate it. He and the Seattle Police Department had quite a history in that respect, as Dylan himself knew—the Taurus .380 which had been taken away just a couple of weeks before, had been registered in Carlson's name. It was also one of the guns which had been temporarily impounded the previous June.

The pair set off for Stan Baker's Gun Shop, on Lake City Way NE—Baker later remembered wondering "what the hell are those kids going to do with that shotgun? It's not hunting season." But it was not his concern, either. Dylan purchased the weapon, a 61b Remington Model 11 20-gauge shotgun, and the two left the store. Dylan later asked Kurt if he wanted him to keep the rifle at his condo. Kurt told him no. That day was to be their last meeting.

Where Kurt went from there may never be known for certain. Later on Wednesday, he was in a downtown gunshop buying a second box of shells. He did spend at least one night at a property he and Courtney had bought the previous year, a little north of Carnation, a township 40 miles northeast of Seattle. Courtney would tell Seattle's *Post Intelligencer* newspaper that it looked as though he'd had company, as well. Balled up by a fireplace, in the still-unfinished two story house which the couple were building, lay a blue sleeping bag which she had never seen before. A nearby ashtray overflowed with cigarette butts—some, she recognized as Kurt's brand, but as for the others, she'd not seen them before either.

On Monday, the day after the private detectives were taken on, Courtney was interviewed by the *L.A. Times'* Robert Hilburn. She spoke of the horror of finding Kurt spread out on the floor in Rome, blue and still. "I don't ever want to see him . . . like that again. I thought I went through a lot of hard times over the years, but [that was] the hardest."

It was the last scheduled interview she would do. The following afternoon, callers were informed by the hotel switchboard that her room was not accepting any calls whatsoever. An interview with the Seattle *Rocket* was cancelled without warning, although Hole guitarist Eric Erlandson explained simply that Courtney was feeling unwell. He promised that he would try to reschedule the telephone interview for later that evening. He didn't.

In fact, Courtney probably wasn't even at the hotel. Instead, she was combing the streets of L.A., searching for her husband.

Back home, Cobain's mother, Wendy O'Connor, was instituting a search of her own, filing a missing person's report with the Seattle police department on Monday. Word had reached her that her son had bought a shotgun; in the report, she described him as armed, and possibly suicidal. But somewhat mysteriously, he was *not* considered dangerous.

Back in L.A., Courtney was voicing similar anxieties. "I'm really afraid for him right now," she told a friend.

In the days that followed, the Seattle police department paid several visits to the Cobains' Madrona home. There was no sign of life. They would also check out the address on Seattle's Capitol Hill, where O'Connor claimed her son bought his drugs. Again, however, there was nothing.

Courtney remained in L.A., wrestling now with both her own conscience and the calm advice of friends. Every instinct in her body was screaming she should return to Seattle to join the search for Kurt. But other people, she admitted later, counselled her simply to sit tight.

They knew as well as she did how volatile Kurt could be when he wanted, how he would so often do one thing when he was asked to do another. The last thing anybody needed was for him to storm off in a fit of contrariness and maybe do something stupid. "I listened to too many people," Courtney confesses. "I'm only going to listen to my gut for the rest of my life."

At the time, however, the advice seemed sensible. The private detectives had apparently made some headway in their search for Kurt—contact had been made, but Kurt refused to be taken back to L.A. Instead, he turned and fled.

He remained in sight, though, and while the idea of physically harnessing Kurt was reluctantly dropped from the gameplan, according to a source, a friend was directed to keep tabs on him.

Also on Monday, a music industry insider is said to have run into Kurt, and pleaded with him to check into a local rehab center. Cobain refused. Other sources claimed to have seen him out in search of drug dealers.

There was even a rumor, reported one week later in the *L.A. Times*, that he actually telephoned a friend to say he'd bought a shotgun. What he needed to know now was, what was the best way to shoot yourself in the head? The friend's response does not appear to have been recorded.

By Tuesday, tension within the Nirvana camp was palpable, although the precise state of affairs remained a closely guarded secret—a decision which may or may not have been wise. It is easy to say that the knowledge that he was the subject of a major private manhunt might simply have driven Kurt further underground. But it is also possible that the more people who searched for him, the more chance there was that someone might find him.

Instead, the only news which had leaked out concerned the aftermath of the unsucessful intervention. Rumors spread first that Gold Mountain had indeed dropped the band from its books, then that Nirvana had just broken up—both possibilities which were only reinforced two days later, when it was announced that contrary to previously published information, Nirvana would *not* be headlining this summer's Lollapalooza tour.

The reason given was Kurt's health problems, although the break-up was just as plausible, particularly— as a few people immediately began speculating—when one considered the apparent ease with which Nirvana had just backed down for the first time from the creative control they had insisted upon when they signed with Geffen.

Although their last album, the six month old *In Utero*, had already sold over two million copies, there were no doubts that it had still to reach its full potential audience. The hoped for reason? The reluctance on the part of so-called rack jobber distributors, to place it into certain "middle America discount chains" on account of its cover art.

A report in the CD newsletter *Ice* announced that a small section of the album's original cover—depicting one of Kurt's own fetus and womb-strewn art works— had been enlarged (the section showed no fetuses) "to serve as the entire back cover . . . [in addition] the song title 'Rape Me' has been changed to read 'Waif Me'."

The report continued, "One Geffen executive estimated that getting the album into [these] stores can add 10% to its total sales figures," meaning "at least 200,000 units are at stake, enough to shake any artist's idealistic stance."

But Kurt was not "any artist", and if his stance could be described as idealistic, it was because his very nature was idealistic. That was what lay at the heart of so many of his problems, a sense, maybe even the knowledge, that all too often, the idealism which he felt simply did not translate into other peoples' worlds.

And though both Geffen and Gold Mountain moved swiftly to defuse the story ("you're really not changing . . . Nirvana's artistic vision," Janet Billig told *Ice*, "just . . . some words on a piece of paper"), few observers could imagine Kurt having simply rolled over and agreed to the butchery of his muse. If nothing else, it did not fit his esprit de punk.

Of course, this may have had nothing to do with the reasons behind the sudden outburst of activity behind the scenes, behind the screens. It really was just another iron lying in the fires of speculation. But there again, so was the very idea that Nirvana were on the verge of splitting up; might even have already done so.

It was not, after all, the first time that a split had seemed imminent. As far back as 1990, Kurt had been threatening to break up the group, as former Nirvana drummer Chad Channing told Seattle journalist Jo-Ann Greene.

"When we were last in Rome together, in 1990, we had an incident . . . where the band was going to break up because we were fed up [with] the way things were going. Kurt just looked at me and said, 'hey, are you still having fun?' "

Those words make for a chilling epitaph—especially after an off-the-record source confessed, that efforts to keep tabs on Kurt had been an abject failure. Three days later it was an electrician, Gary Smith, who finally found him. Are you still having fun?

Sometime on Tuesday, April 5th, Kurt headed back to Madrona, quietly letting himself into the gray house. According to the *Seattle Post Intelligencer*, he was high, riding on the combination of heroin and valium which seemed to blot out his personal pain better than anything else. The *P-I* alleged that the level of smack in his bloodstream was 1.52mg per liter. Doses one third as strong have been known to prove fatal.

The house was silent, empty, dark—it always was when Courtney and Frances were away, and he switched the television on. Then, he slipped across to the mother-in-law apartment above the garage, where Michael De-Witt, Frances Bean's former nanny, had once lived.

His pen recorded his last known thoughts in red ink. "I haven't felt the excitement of listening to, as well as creating music, along with really writing something, for too many years now." He felt tremendously guilty about that. The screaming crowds didn't excite him, he said, as they did Freddie Mercury, who appeared to love and relish the love and adoration of the crowd. Which is something I totally admire and envy, the fact that I can't fool you, any one of you. It simply isn't fair to you or to me . . ."

"There's good in all of us, and I simply love people too much. So much that it makes me feel just too fucking sad. Sad, little, sensitive, unappreciated, Pisces, Jesus man."

"I had a good marriage, and for that I'm grateful. But since the age of seven, I've become hateful toward all humans in general, only because it seems so easy for people to get along . . . empathy. . . . Thank you all from the pit of my burning, nauseous stomach for your letters and concerns during the last years. I'm too much of an erratic, moody person, and I don't have the passion anymore."

Then a line from a Neil Young song came to mind, from "Hey Hey, My My" . . . "it's better to burn out than to fade away." He wrote it down. "So remember, it's better to burn out than fade away."

Finally, he was done. He signed off—"Love, peace and empathy, Kurt Cobain"—and stabbed his pen through the letter, and impaled it into a planter. And then he reached for his shotgun.

2

A couple of hours southwest of Seattle, Aberdeen had very little time indeed for whatever was going on in the city. The miles which separate the two might have easily been translated into worlds, even galaxies. While Seattle grew, proudly blossoming beneath its reputation as America's most liveable city, Aberdeen clung tighter and tighter to a life which grew weaker with every passing year.

It is a logging and fishing community, ringed by the forests which years of woodcutting have finally reduced to near-nothing, fringed by an ocean which has been trawled into a desert. Trailer parks pockmark Route 12 into town, trickling slowly into fast food hell, which in turn is succeeded by the scars of recession—locked-up houses, closed-down stores, and everywhere, reminders of how precarious life in small town America can be.

House after house has the same sign in the windows, "This family is supported by timber dollars"; car after car sports a bumper sticker damning the day God ever created the Spotted Owl. There is a sickening irony in the survival of one creature being dependent upon the extinction of another, but that was the reality which faced the Federal Government. When the owl won out over logging, the undertakers moved that little bit closer to Aberdeen, WA. And with good cause. As employment dipped, suicides climbed, until Grays Harbor County could boast one of the highest rates in America.

In their own way, Nirvana restored some pride to this crumbling remnant of a once-vibrant community. It doesn't matter that even on the day his death was discovered, there was little outward activity to suggest that this day was different from any other day; nor does it matter what the townsfolk's own memories of the "Cobain kid" were; still there was a sense that Nirvana had returned Aberdeen to a map which the last few years had seemed set to wipe it off of.

A couple of other bands had escaped Aberdeen before them, the Melvins and Metal Church, and both had done pretty well for themselves—Church even notched up a few hundred thousand record sales. But neither had done as well as Nirvana, neither had drawn not only reporters, but fans, by the car-load, by the bus-load, into the town to poke, gawk and chatter. Boston has its Paul Revere, Stratford has its Shakespeare. Aberdeen had Nirvana.

It did not even seem to matter that for Kurt Cobain and Chris Novoselic, the years they'd spent in Aberdeen were years they would rather forget; that they had escaped Aberdeen's cloistered, claustrophobic red-neckery at the first opportunity they got. In the months which followed Nirvana's initial national breakthrough, while the nation's press was beating a camera-strewn path to the heart of Aberdeen, visitors were greeted with open arms, and wide open mouths.

When Patrick MacDonald, rock critic for the *Seattle Times*, visited Aberdeen in early 1992, he was led on a grand tour of *Cobainiana*, everything from the bridge he used to sleep beneath, to the demolished amplifier he left behind when he split. Such relics had a resonance which was pure rock'n'roll. But if you really wanted to talk stock cliches, they were more a symbol of a true teenage wasteland. From where Kurt stood, even the dim lights of Olympia glowed like beacons in an endless night.

Although he was to live there for more than two-thirds of his life, Kurt Donald Cobain was not a true Aberdeen native; rather, he was born in neighboring Hoquiam, a town which arguably has even less of a past to be proud of than Aberdeen.

At least Aberdeen had a railroad, an iron route out of the glowering forests, and until a mid-1950s police crackdown finally crushed the life from the ladies, it also had brothels, upwards of fifty in the downtown alone. A decade later, the place was clean, but its reputation lingered, not as the festering scab which some latter-day writers have termed it, but as another point of local light, something soft and nostalgic which could still fill an empty night.

Donald Cobain and his wife, Wendy Fradenburg left Hoquiam with their six-month-old son during the summer of 1967. Kurt had been born on February 20th; three years later, he would have a sister, Kimberley, but right now, in the rented house where he spent his first months, and the mortgaged home where his mother still lives, he was the center of the Cobain family's universe—particularly Wendy's.

To his death, Kurt remembered the amazement he felt when he learned that not every child grows up with a mother who always kissed him and hugged him goodbye when he went out to play. "There's nothing like your first-born—nothing," Wendy told journalist Michael Azerrad. "No child never even comes close to that. I was totaled out on him. My every waking hour was for him."

Kurt's mother was not alone with those feelings, however. There was something compulsive about the child, an energy, a dynamism, a sense of explosive precocity which neither she, nor anybody she knew, had ever before encountered in one so young. On at least one occasion, in conversation with her own mother, Wendy admitted that Kurt's perceptiveness almost scared her, and when the boy was excited—as he so often seemed to be—it was all she and Don could do to control him.

It was to quell this hyperactivity that the boy was prescribed ritalin, an amphetamine-based drug which has been proven an effective weapon against excessive energy in children. In Kurt's case, however, the tablets had an effect even more excessive than his "normal" behavior, frequently keeping him up and active until the small hours of the morning.

The treatment was halted, and sedatives substituted for speed. Now, he slept in school. Finally, it was suggested that Kurt's parents take that most drastic step of all—remove sugar from Kurt's diet. It was, his relieved parents were finally able to say, third time lucky.

This restrictive new diet quieted Kurt, but it did not slow him down. He was everywhere at once, getting into trouble whenever and wherever possible, and if he wasn't, then Boda was. Boda, Kurt would proudly explain, was his friend, an invisible ball of irrepressible energy, and it didn't matter what went wrong around the house, what latest piece of mischief could be tracked back to Kurt, Kurt always had his answer waiting on his lips. "It wasn't me who did it, it was Boda."

"It just became ridiculous," Wendy later recalled—Boda even demanded his own place setting at the meal table!

Finally, Kurt's Uncle Clark hit on a solution. A soldier, he asked Kurt if he could take Boda to Vietnam with him to keep him company. Kurt looked at his Uncle quizzically, then very seriously led his mother to one side.

"Boda isn't real," he whispered. "Does Clark know that?"

It is one of the greatest cliches in the annals of showbusiness to describe a person as a "born performer," even more so when it is applied retrospectively to the performer as a child. But Wendy insists that with Kurt, that indeed was the case, and she had seven brothers and sisters who would vouchsafe her word—to the point of actually volunteering to babysit the child, just so he could entertain them with his antics.

Barely could Kurt walk and talk, than his delighted uncles and aunts were pinpointing his brightest characteristics, and having vied for the privilege of having him visit, now they sportingly argued over who he most closely resembled.

Taking it for granted that he was a talented toddler; accepting that the delight he took in music was the hallmark of a deeper ability, one could argue that when it came to plucking role models from within his immediate family, Kurt was spoiled for choice.

Everybody, it seemed, played a musical instrument of some sort—Wendy's brother Chuck even played in a real rock'n'roll band, and made the first ever tape of Kurt Cobain singing, a song which became a chorus of "poo-poo"s, recorded when Kurt was just four. Aunt Mary was a country singer, and had a recording studio in one room of her house. Wendy herself had once dreamed of becoming a drummer. And bestriding them all like a spangled colossus was their uncle, Delbert Fradenburg. Early in the 1940s, he split Aberdeen for the bright lights of L.A., changed his name to the decidedly more stylish-sounding Dale Arden, and even cut a few records. The others in the family were talents to be sure. But Uncle Delbert, he'd been a star.

If music became Kurt's first passion, by the time he hit seven, art was his second. The only problem was, although he loved to paint and draw, he never seemed to like what he'd done. When the school newspaper extended to the chubby second grader an honor which rarely went to anyone below the fifth grade, supplying a drawing for the cover one issue, Kurt's reaction was one of outrage, disgust. The picture really wasn't that good, he insisted—how could the school show him up like this?

"His attitude toward adults changed because of that," his mother later mourned. They were telling him how much they loved his art, and Kurt simply didn't believe them, couldn't believe them, because he himself "was never satisfied with it". Even at that early age, Kurt seemed wise, and with that wisdom, sensitive beyond his years.

His inquisitive eyes, already capable of piercing to the soul of whosoever he was talking with, would scan that person for signs of insincerity, a psychic radar which cornered condescension and repaid it with disdain. Wendy admits that from the moment Kurt's artistic talents were first noticed, the entire family engulfed him in supplies, until "it kind of got crammed down his throat. We . . . almost killed it for him."

But was it the attention which turned him away from his art, the pressures of his presupposed accomplishment? Or the knowledge, bubbling within his soul, that if he was to follow his abilities in any direction whatsoever, it was music which would make him, not art.

Even to a seven-year-old, it was impossible not to become somehow swept along by the excitement of rock'n'roll. To a seven-year-old whose own family was actively thrusting that music in his face, the impossibility was magnified manifold.

The first records Kurt ever owned were gifts from his Aunt Mary—after Great Uncle Delbert, the family's other pop superstar. Mary played guitar in a country band, regularly performed in Aberdeen's bars, and once even released a record. Visiting her house as he so often did, Kurt was thrilled to hear her play it, to watch the little 45 spinning around on the player, and know that his own aunt could be heard playing on it. At seven or eight, gramophone records are still the stuff of dreams, a romantic mystery into whose secrets only the luckiest of the lucky can ever be inducted. Simply to be related to one of those people seemed a dream come true.

It was Mary who first offered Kurt guitar lessons, but although the boy appeared keen to learn, had few toys he loved more than his little plastic guitar, the rigidity of even the simplest lessons sent him hurtling, bored senseless, toward whichever distraction presented itself to him. In the end, she gave up trying, and let him simply amuse himself. And that was no problem, because he was *such* a happy child.

Kurt himself later agreed. Smiling at what now seemed a joyously uncomplicated memory, he remarked, "I was constantly screaming and singing. I didn't know when to quit." The other children at school even took to beating him up, simply to keep him quiet!

Aunt Mary thought about another solution, but there would be many times, maybe, when Kurt's mother and father wished that she hadn't. Anything would have been better than the damnable bass drum she bought him.

Sliding his tiny feet into his father's tennis shoes, planting a hunting cap over his head, Kurt would strap on his treasured drum and set out around the neighborhood, banging and crashing and accompanying himself with Beatles songs. That was Aunt Mary's doing as well, the Beatles and the Monkees, and though Kurt still strummed his plastic guitar, and leaped around his bedroom like he'd seen pop stars do on television, it was the drums which fascinated him now.

Wendy encouraged him in this latest love, just as she'd encouraged his others. As Kurt entered third grade, he began taking drum lessons, then he'd go home from the after-school classes, and continue the lessons alone. Though he never would learn to read music, he swiftly discovered that his natural abilities as a musician were complimented by a talent for mimicry, too. As soon as one person in the class learned a piece of music, Kurt would be copying them, and playing it better as well.

This ideal world, the loving family, the household in which nothing seemed too much trouble, or even too expensive, came crashing down around Kurt's ears in 1975.

It was difficult to tell when things started going wrong between Don and Wendy Cobain—outwardly, despite Kurt's later condemnations ("white trash posing as middle class"), theirs' was the model of working class suburban gentility, a nice home fixed up until it dwarfed its run-down neighbors, a father whose livelihood was not rooted in wood (Don was a motor mechanic, working at the local Chevron gas station), a model mother homemaker, children who always turned out clean and clean-smelling.

But behind the facade, the foundations of marriage were rotten. Don, Wendy complained, never seemed to be home anymore—he always seemed to be off, playing sports or coaching them, then coming home exhausted and sleeping till the alarm clock announced another working day. Calm regret became bitter resentment; sometimes, Wendy would wonder whether she had ever truly loved her husband, and though they tried to keep their lives together afloat, sometime after Kurt's eighth birthday, his parents finally separated.

And a light went out in Kurt's life forever.

Divorce is traditionally among the most traumatic events a child can experience, the sundering of the principle point of stability in a young life and its sudden replacement by the twin burdens of guilt and responsibility which the child will frequently automatically shoulder; a sense that somehow, *it was all my fault*.

For Kurt, those pains were exaggerated not only by his youthful failure to understand the true reasons for the breakdown of his parents' marriage, and by the drawn-out divorce proceedings which followed, but also by his own personal failings, those which Kurt himself must have considered of immense importance.

His father was an avid sportsman, and like so many dads, would have liked nothing more than to see his son follow in his footsteps. But Kurt had no interest whatsoever in sport. Was it his failure to excel . . . no, hang "excel"; his failure to show even the slightest glimmer of enthusiasm for batting a rock-hard ball around a field which forced his father away from the family home, and into a prefab in a trailer park in Montesano? Had the anger which would explode from his father on the occasions that Kurt *did* join in a team sport, only to strike out the first time he moved, had it finally got too much?

Maybe it was Kurt's refusal—again against his father's dearest wishes—to do with his right hand what came easiest with his left. Believing, rightly or wrongly, that left-handedness places a child at a disadvantage, Don worked hard to encourage Kurt to switch sides. He failed, as so many similarly inclined parents fail, because nature will seldom allow herself to be thwarted. But Kurt didn't know that. He just knew that he did things wrong. Perhaps *that* was why dad left home?

Was it his inability to behave, as his mother later said, like the "little adult" which his father demanded? If he closed his eyes and thought real hard, Kurt could easily summon up the feelings of pain and confusion which coursed through his body every time his father called him a dummy, rapped him across the knuckles, or around the head. But he'd deserved that treatment, because he was stupid or rude, and maybe dad was gone because of that, too.

Or maybe, lastly, it was the events of Christmas, 1974, which placed the last straw on the camel's creaking back. Kurt had asked for a toy gun, one which was neatly packaged in the names of Starsky and Hutch, the derring-do cops whose plain-clothes activities dominated the prime time television listings. It cost $5, but it was worth the money—or so Kurt thought.

Wendy disagreed, and when Kurt came down on Christmas morning, and found the heavy, bulky package which lay beneath the tree, he had no idea what it could be. It didn't feel like a Starsky and Hutch gun, and as he ran his hands over the nobbly, even grainy surface . . . in fact it felt like . . . slowly, Kurt opened the neatly wrapped gift. It was a lump of coal. That had been his mother's way of punishing him for being greedy. Maybe leaving was dad's way of doing it.

Back in his bedroom, Kurt wrote what might well be the earliest piece of his poetry still in existence today. He scrawled it on the wall:

"I hate Mom, I hate Dad

"Dad hates Mom, Mom hates Dad

"It simply makes you want to be so sad."

For the next year or so, Kurt lived on in Aberdeen with his mother and sister Kimberley. But the divorce had changed him, from the always bright, always happy child who had once so delighted his family and friends, to a withdrawn, sullen, rude little boy, who took his private rage out on whatever, whoever got in his way. He locked his babysitters out of the house, and argued constantly with both his mother and her new boyfriend, who he believed was "a mean huge wife-beater." Finally, Wendy could take no more. Kurt was passed on to his father, in the trailer park in Montesano.

There, Kurt and his father worked hard, and apparently successfully, to repair the breaches which Kurt had discerned in their earlier relationship. The boy's every whim was indulged—Don bought him a motorized minibike, accompanied him camping in the vast state park which stretches up the Olympia Peninsula; took him to the long, lonely beaches which line the Pacific coast. Don even tried to take Kurt hunting, although on that occasion, Kurt's interest died once they reached the forest. Somehow, killing animals for fun just didn't seem to be any . . . fun. Still, Don later said, "he had everything. He had it made."

Don was now working as a tallyman for the Mayer Brothers logging company, checking inventory. His hours were difficult—he often had to work clear through the weekend, but Kurt was always welcome to join him at the yard, to amuse himself in the warehouse, playing amidst the newly-cut wood, or sit in Don's office, making crank calls to the numbers he'd dial at random.

Then it would be out to Don's van to play 8-Track tapes on the car stereo. With the unquenchable enthusiasm of a child, he could happily listen to the same album over and over, sitting through the constant rumble of the tape machine's capstans and rollers, the thunderous clunk at the end of each tape length, until it appeared that even these extraneous noises were an integral part of the music.

His favorite album, as 1977 came to a close, was Queen's *News of the World*, with the anthemic signature tune which was already swamping the sports stadia of America, "We Are The Champions". For hours in the truck, he would play it, often until the van's battery was exhausted, just sitting there punching buttons on the in-dash tape player so that the tape would return to the beginning each time, and he knew every word off by heart.

Slowly, it appeared, Kurt was rehabilitating himself within at least one half of his family. Long father-son discussions helped exorcise some of the guilt he felt over his parents' divorce, as Don patiently explained that sometimes, people simply fall out of love, that it is nobody's fault and no one's to blame. It's just that feelings they had when they were younger can change.

And there was something else which Don said, that made an impression on Kurt's slowly calming mind. The actual conversation is forgotten, but the gist of it was, as

Kurt would bitterly remember for the remainder of his life, Don said he would never remarry.

So when he turned around, in February, 1978, and did just that, Kurt was shattered—and two years of coming to terms with his new life were undone at a stroke.

Suddenly, all the old feelings of insecurity and doubt flooded back, and with them, the long-learned lessons that you could never, ever, trust an adult.

Kurt, Don, his new wife, and her two children, moved across town, away from the trailer park and into a real house. Kurt hated all of it. When his step-mother tried to work things out with him, kindly at first, but with understandable, increasing frustration, Kurt threw her concern back in her face. The three children—Kurt, his step-brother and step-sister—each had household chores designated for them. Kurt's invariably went sur-lily undone. He started missing school, and when Don found him a part-time job bussing tables at a nearby restaurant, Kurt simply ignored it altogether.

He bullied his younger step-siblings, and when Don asked if Kurt wanted to join the family shopping at the mall, the boy would storm out of sight, down to the basement room he had taken as his own, and that just made things even worse. When the others got back, there would invariably be a bright new toy for them to play with. Kurt got nothing.

Desperately, even angrily, Don persuaded Kurt to join the school wrestling team. If that didn't curb, or at least exhaust, the boy's constant aggression, what would?

Kurt hated it, but despite that, he was a useful fighter. Stocky, stubborn, and considerably stronger than his still-sensitive features would ever let on, Kurt simply lulled his opponents into a false sense of security, until the moment he pounced, and suddenly the realization would strike everyone simultaneously. The boy looked like an angel, but he fought like the devil—when he wanted to, at least.

Larry Smith, Kurt's step-uncle, recalls hearing one day that Kurt was involved in a fight with "a burly 250 lb. logger type." But "Kurt didn't even fight. He just presented the bully with the appropriate hand gesture every time he was knocked down, until the bully gave up. To top it all off, Kurt just had that usual grin on his face."

Wrestling did not curb Kurt's angry behavior. He started hankering to move back to Aberdeen, to his mother and her boyfriend, and that just pushed an even greater wedge between father and son. Only a couple of years before that Kurt was complaining that he *couldn't* live with her any longer. Now, all of a sudden, she was the greatest thing in his world.

Don resisted Kurt's struggles. Desperate to bring the boy back into his household, under his, Don's, own terms, the elder Cobain applied for—and was granted— legal custody of his son. But it didn't help; if anything, it simply encouraged Kurt toward even more rebellious behavior.

Still it was ironic that when the inevitable break between father and son finally came, it was Kurt's wrestling which provoked it.

He had reached the championship stage of a school wrestling competition, and Don was as proud as any father could be. There was no doubt in his mind that Kurt would win the fight, bringing glory to himself and his family. Kurt, too, seemed confident. It wasn't until the two fighters were on the mats, on their hands and knees awaiting the referee's whistle, that maybe Don sensed that things were not going to go as planned. There was something about the way Kurt looked him straight in the eye, smiled . . . and kept smiling, even as the whistle blew, and his opponent flattened him.

"You should have seen the look on his face," Kurt

told writer Michael Azerrad. "He actually walked out halfway through the match because I did it . . . four times in a row." Immediately after, Kurt went to stay with an uncle and aunt for a time.

He returned to Montesano after what can best be described as a cooling off period, and immediately resumed the tentative dance with his father, courting one another's approval even as they rejected each other's values. What was sad was that most of the time, they weren't even aware they were doing it!

One classic example occurred after one of Don's friends persuaded him to join the Columbia House record and tape club—so many albums or 8-Tracks for a penny, and thereafter, just a few more to buy at regular prices, over the next few years. Maybe the friend was already a member, chasing the Club's offer of further free records for anybody introducing new members; Don went along with the idea anyway, and it soon became obvious that Kurt was showing an interest.

But instead of sharing his son's enthusiasm, Don's interest in the Club's offers swiftly waned. He kept paying the bills, but he rarely played the records. They were just something which kept the boy quiet.

Regularly, the mailman would bring another package to the door, addressed to Don but to be opened by Kurt, and slowly the boy's interest in music began to develop way beyond the Beatles and Monkees albums which Aunt Mary had given him years before. They were simply kids' stuff, like . . . like the music listened to by the others in Kurt's fourth grade class at school. When he talked about his latest acquisition, albums by Led Zeppelin, Black Sabbath or Kiss, they just yawned. That Cobain kid had always been weird—his classmates simply let him get on with it.

Instead, Kurt turned toward another crowd entirely, junior high kids with feather cut hair and ragged rock'n'-roll T-shirts, wasters dragging their way through school *en route* to a job pumping gas or peddling burgers. Kurt adored them, Don—at the very best—tolerated them, and turned a blind eye to the increasingly bizarre-looking magazines which were suddenly being left around the house.

When Kurt was 10 years old, in 1977, he discovered the American music press, around the same time as *it* discovered Punk Rock—the snarling bastard mutant which had erupted from the English streets a year before, and was now embracing America's youth in the same spittle-soaked tentacles as it had grasped its own countrymen.

If Aberdeen was hardly a center of musical innovation—the single record store in town carried little more than one would expect to find in any out-of-the-way township, the *Billboard* Top 40 and the back catalog biggies—Montesano was even further from the hub. There wasn't even one record store there, while the news stands catered to the commonest denominator there was—guns, hunting and baseball, and in the section labeled music, *Creem* and *Rolling Stone*.

Kurt gravitated towards *Creem*. It was a handy size to roll up in one pocket, it didn't get lost in left-wing politics, and best of all, it was littered with photographs, weird photos, wild photos, photos of people with names like Johnny Rotten and Sid Vicious, Iggy Pop and Richard Hell.

It was a little piece of New York, a tasty mouthful of London, flattened into color print and shipped right across the country to feed Kurt's fervent imagination. It didn't even matter that Kurt had never heard a Punk Rock record, that he had no idea what this new music sounded like. Just looking at the pictures, he could imagine it. It was a scream of defiance, of anger and pain, a cacophonous magic which could cure every ill.

As he entered his teens, emboldened even further by his new friends, Kurt finally embarked upon the weary nomadic course which had been threatening throughout the last few years. A succession of relatives took turns boarding him, some certainly wondering what they could have ever found so enchanting about the unruly little monster which Kurt had become. Passed between three aunts and uncles, and on to Don's parents, the most constant feature in Kurt's life seemed to be his suitcase. He once claimed to have moved from Montesano to Aberdeen at least twice a year, until he was 13 and Wendy stepped back in.

She had finally broken up with the boyfriend, freed herself from the cycle of physical and mental abuse which had all but become her everyday life. But she wasn't working any longer, and she simply couldn't afford to raise a growing boy right then. Instead, she suggested he move in with Uncle Chuck, the family rock'n'roller. Kurt agreed like a shot.

Like Don, Chuck had a fabulous record collection. Unlike Don, he actually played the records, listened to them and loved them. The quest for musical knowledge which the Montesano wasters had instilled into Kurt in their own drunken fashion went into overdrive.

Chuck was well aware just how prodigious a musical awareness was bursting inside his young nephew, and did his level best to encourage it. But he had learned from the family's past mistakes. Gifts to Kurt would be presented not as *fait accompli*, like the hailstorm of paint sets which pounded the six-year-old artist into disgruntled submission, but as choices. "Hey, what do you want for your birthday?" he asked, as Kurt's 14th year loomed closer and closer. "A bicycle? Or an electric guitar?"

Kurt was impressed. A choice? You mean, it didn't matter either way? He grabbed the guitar, a barely serviceable used Sears model, and a battered 10 watt amplifier. Then, picking up from where Aunt Mary left off, but substituting her patient description of chords and progressions for the roaring thunder of raw Heavy

Metal, Kurt asked one of Chuck's bandmates, Warren
Mason, if he'd teach him to play "Back in Black"—AC/
DC's howling tribute to their late vocalist, Bon Scott.

Even though he barely understood it himself, there
was a primal poetry to the song, a sense that if you could
master its chords, you never needed any others. "I found
out about power chords. With power chords, you could
play just about anything."

Before long, Kurt was playing the Cars' "Best Friend's
Girl" and Queen's funk heavy "Another One Bites the
Dust". He had also figured out "Louie Louie", Richard
Berry's garage punk anthem, a staple of every band's
repertoire, it seemed since time began.

His horizons had broadened since those days he spent
leafing through the Columbia House catalog, circling the
band names which sounded the wildest, just as his
experiences had widened since the days when he stared
at pictures of Punk Rock, and dreamed of how it must
sound.

Watching *Saturday Night Live*, he'd stared in amazement at the musical guests who rolled through the
studios. When the Athens, GA, art-quintet B52s appeared, performing "Rock Lobster" in mid-1980, he may
have squirmed at their quaintness, but he fell in love
with their spirit, and went head-over-heels at the sight
of vocalist Fred Schneider's shoes, checkerboard Vans
which were simply so neat. The next day, Kurt patiently
painted black and white squares on his sneakers.

But the B52s were simply the tip of the iceberg.
Across America, infiltrating even into the backwater
boondocks of wildest Washington State, the Punk bands
who had mutated into the New Wave were now turning
up everywhere. Kurt heard the Ramones, and was heart-
broken when he discovered that they had once played
Aberdeen, four leather-clad New Yorkers whose songs
were played faster than bassist Dee Dee could count
them in, jack-hammering through their teenaged an-

thems before a half-empty room of increasingly agitated
drunk loggers. Kurt remembered the date—March 5th,
1977, the day Punk Rock came to Aberdeen, then turned
right around and left it again. Privately, he made a vow
to himself—the next time Punk showed its face on those
streets, he'd be there to make sure it stayed.

The Clash had a new album out, a fat triple album
they called *Sandinista*. Kurt bought it because the Clash
. . . they were there at the beginning, with the Pistols
on tour, and the first night of the Roxy, bellowing
napalm and slogans and mantras to a future which had
once been unimaginable . . . "no Elvis, Beatles or
the Rolling Stones". Back home, flushed, excited, he
dropped the album onto his turntable . . . and it could
have been Uncle Chuck, it could have been Aunt Mary.
It could have been anyone, but it wasn't Punk. Or at
least, it wasn't the Punk he heard in his head.

Fourteen years old, with an electric guitar, a repertoire
which grew around the blistered remnants of FM radio
classics, Kurt figured that if Punk wouldn't come to him,
he'd go to it. "Three chords and a lot of screaming",
that's all it took, and upstairs in his bedroom he would
cauterize the walls with his noise, his tiny, tinny amplifier shaking its guts out while Kurt thrashed his guitar,
wrestling it, wringing its scrawny fretboard neck. "It
was definitely a good release."

3

That was the first thing Kurt Cobain ever wanted to be as a child, then—a rock star. He thought about running for President, but "that was a stupid idea." He'd much rather be a rock star.

That idea lasted until he was eight or nine, and he saw the stuntman, Evel Knievel, on television. The guy was fearless. Revving up his motorbike, already precariously balanced on a narrow plank roadway, many feet up in the air, Knievel would launch himself skyward, man and machine in anti-gravity free-fall, over the rows of parked school buses, cars and lorries, whatever lay in his way. Then, effortlessly, faultlessly, he would touch down on the far side of the gulf, on another narrow plank, and he'd cruise calmly back to earth, smiling quietly to himself as though he couldn't understand the fuss. Heck, don't people do this all the time?

Kurt didn't know, but he thought that they should . . . he thought that he should. In the woods around his home, he would arrange obstacle courses that he would have to negotiate, and he was obstinate enough that no number of bruises, cuts, scrapes and pains could deter him. One day, he wrestled his bicycle onto a low roof, climbed aboard and sailed into the garden. Another time, he threw all his bedding onto the deck below his bedroom window, then leaped into it from the first floor. He wondered how it would feel to explode, so he taped firecrackers to a sheet of metal, then taped that onto his chest. The ensuing explosion almost deafened him, but he lived. Yeah, he wanted to be a stuntman.

Now, with Punk Rock coursing through his veins, howling in his head, he was back to being a rock star again, but a Punk Rock star, and he knew just the people to help him do it.

Back living with Don, Kurt had patiently submitted to his father's demands that he join the Babe Ruth League baseball team. It seemed a total waste of time—Kurt loathed the game, found it futile and boring, and on the occasions when he was called to bat, it was the easiest thing in the world to swing his stick around incompetently, and wait till he struck out. Then it was back to the bench, and more time to talk music with Matt Lukin.

Lukin was a rarity at Montesano High, a person with whom Kurt clicked almost as soon as they met, in electronics class. He was into Kiss and Cheap Trick, bands which may have defied Kurt's taste in Punk, but had a certain snottiness anyway. Kiss were still wearing make-up in those days, fire-breathing drag which might have been corny, may have been shtick, but was a lot more exciting than most of what was going on then.

Even better, though, Lukin was in a rock band, and not an all-adults bar band like Chuck and Warren Mason, but a savage, blazing brat band, turning out covers of old Who and Hendrix, but impaling them on an enthusiasm which the original songwriters would have scarcely re-membered. They were called the Melvins.

One evening, Kurt dropped by one of their rehearsals, the first real rock band he had ever seen in person. It was before he met Lukin; Kurt went along at the invitation of a friend of a friend of the Melvins' first drummer, Mike

Dillard. He wasn't even in ninth grade yet, either, but he was horribly, embarrassingly drunk on wine.

He told the band they were wonderful about a million times, and was thrown out of the room in return. As he climbed down from the attic where the Melvins rehearsed, he lost his footing and slipped. His first rock'n'-roll show, and if he'd not been so drunk, it would have hurt like hell.

The Melvins were fronted by Buzz Osbourne, a few years Kurt's senior, and already an imposing sight. Like Kurt, he didn't so much play his guitar as manhandle it, thumping out his riffs, but skewing them slightly into something all his own. And already, he had shown that Montesano was not the be-all and end-all of his universe.

Osbourne had been to Seattle a few times, to see other bands or to gig with his own; to Kurt, that was the peak of achievement, and the older boy—he wasn't a Montesano schoolkid, he was a guru.

Osbourne met Cobain's adulation with friendship. That unfortunate evening in the attic aside, there was something innately fascinating about the unruly boy with the wild hair and piercing eyes. "When I first met Kurt Cobain, he looked like a teenage runaway," Osbourne said years later. Then, reflecting on the image which by then was stapled all across the country—"come to think of it, he still does."

Watching Kurt in class, Osbourne would also watch the trail of graffiti'd devastation which the boy left behind him, carving the Sex Pistols' logo into every available surface. One day, Buzz arrived at school with a Sex Pistols photo book—"Kurt, you can borrow this, if you like!" Osbourne could have disappeared the very next day, and he would still have been Kurt's friend for life. As it was, Osbourne had a few more treats up his sleeve.

In terms of his musical education, Osbourne wasn't that different from Kurt Cobain. He was brought up on a diet of '70s metal—"Aerosmith, Ted Nugent, things like that," only for Punk to wipe the slate clean in much the same way as it affected any "reasonably aware, reasonably curious, 14- or 15-year-old.

"I bought the Sex Pistols album (*Never Mind the Bollocks, Here's the Sex Pistols*) out of curiosity, to find out what people who looked like [they did] could sound like."

It was "the energy and the aggression" which affected him most, the amphetamine roar of the guitars which introduce "Anarchy in the U.K.", the stumbling sub-Stooges motif of "Submission", the blatant moron chanting of "I'm A Lazy Sod (17)" and "Pretty Vacant". The music seemed "so uncontrolled, but [it had] such a tight musical focus. It was so different from anything I had ever heard before.

"Then I met someone who had [a collection of] British Punk records—the Vibrators, 999, Buzzcocks, stuff I'd never heard of." It was that which allowed him to sort out "in my own mind, the stuff I wanted to live with—and the stuff I could live without. That collection was my education", and that was what he would be sharing with Kurt.

Up late playing records, Buzz would make cassettes for Kurt to listen to, Southern California hardcore bands like Flipper, MDC, Black Flag, the Circle Jerks, purveyors of a music whose reputations were so wild, whose audiences were so violent, that the Huntington Beach police department actually started classifying some punk bands as gangs, and their fans as gang members. During the periodic clampdowns on the public show of gang colors, you could get run in as easily for wearing a punk-rock T-shirt as you could for sporting a Bloods or Crips leather.

He and Kurt started going to shows together; the first one Kurt remembered was Vancouver's D.O.A., the missing link—as their own geography demanded—

between L.A. hardcore and Anglo-East Coast snottiness. The second was Black Flag. Tickets for the show at the Mountaineers Club on Seattle's 3rd Ave cost $12, and Kurt sold his entire record collection, every last Foreigner, Kiss and Pat Benatar album he owned, simply for one night of frenzied noise and vicious slam dancing.

But it was worth it. After hearing Black Flag in full spiteful flight, vocalist Henry Rollins confronting his audience with the worst fears that their parents could dream of, who could ever go back to the sanitized bleating of Journey and Co.? The next day, sometime around the middle of August, 1984, Kurt spiked his hair "and started spray-painting people's cars. I claimed I would forever be a Punk!"

"Punk Rock is about total rejects," says Mudhoney's Steve Turner. "If you see a bunch of guys on the stage that look like 'rock' people, you say 'oh, a rock band.' It's far scarier to see total freaks up there going AAAAAARRRRUUUGGGHHH!"

It was the AAAAAARRRRUUUGGGHHH! which most appealed to Kurt, the primal therapy of society's disenfranchised disgorging itself through one throat-scourging yell. He had already learned about power chords; now Kurt was discovering power screams. Out fishing with his step-uncle Larry one day, Kurt didn't dip his rod in the water the whole time he lay by the river. He just leaned back on the bank and screamed. When Larry came over and asked what was wrong, Kurt simply smiled. "Nothing. I'm just strengthening my vocal chords."

Now Kurt was telling told Osbourne that he was thinking of starting a Punk Rock band, that it was going to be the best fucking Punk Rock band in the world. Osbourne was in no doubt that he *could* do it. The question was, did he really *want* to?

"I couldn't relate to people at all," Kurt later imparted.

"So I basically hung out by myself all the time, and played guitar."

He enjoyed his self-imposed confinement, particularly when whichever relation he was living with respected, or at least accepted, that the strange boy upstairs was never going to snap out of it and start behaving normally. When Kurt did appear downstairs, it was generally either to grab something out of the fridge, or be on his way out with his friends. Clearly he was unhappy, but what could they do? What could *he* do?

The previous May, Kurt's mother had remarried. Pat O'Connor was a hard drinking longshoreman, and when Kurt first asked if he could come back to live in the house he'd grown up in, her first response was to tell him there was simply no way that could happen. It took Kurt "months" to change her mind, staying on the telephone for as long as he could, crying, pleading, begging. Finally, Wendy relented, but for both Kurt and his mother, their reunion was to remain a double-edged sword.

For Kurt, the hardest thing was to see the way Pat treated his mother. In one oft-related incident, O'Connor stayed out all night long, finally arriving home at 7 A.M., roaring drunk from the arms of another woman. Wendy bit her tongue and left for work as usual, but there was no escape. "Hey! Where was Pat last night?" A couple of O'Connor's drinking buddies were hanging around the department store, and the leer in the voice made it plain that they knew the answer just as well as she.

Wendy called a friend, and the pair went out and got drunk. Then she stormed home.

Pat was downstairs with Kurt and Kimberley as Wendy walked into the house, went to the closet and pulled out one of her husband's guns, threatening to shoot him. She wrestled with the weapon, trying to figure out how to load it; when she realized that she couldn't, she simply gathered up every gun in the house—and there was a lot of them, Pat was a keen hunter and collector; had Kim collect together all the ammunition she could find, and they dumped the whole lot in the Wishkah River.

Watching from his bedroom window, Kurt's mind was already ticking over, how to turn this latest domestic crisis to his own, personal advantage. Some people reckon the story starts edging into apocryphy here, but that doesn't really matter. Kurt told it like it was true.

The moment the coast was clear, he rounded up a couple of neighborhood kids, handed them a few bucks, and told them to dredge the river for weapons. Then, once they'd collected as many as they could, he hauled the whole lot downtown and sold them.

A guy in town had an amplifier for sale. Kurt bought the amp, then suggested that the two of them head out and get some pot. Only Kurt didn't have any more money, on account of having just bought the amp, but the seller was feeling particularly flush, and told him not to worry. The way Kurt told the tale, the guy blew his entire wad on pot, and not only did Kurt get a new amplifier, he also got stoned in the process.

For a long time, Kurt had amazed his friends by *not* indulging in the vices which made Aberdeen seem at least vaguely tolerable. He was already suffering from many of the ailments which would conspire to make his adulthood so painful—the bronchitis which had dogged him since he was a toddler, the mysterious gastric agonies which could make him cough up blood and dream of suicide, the nerve-burning back ache. He already had to be so careful what he ate—he was even more careful about what else he put in his body. "Kurt . . . was the only young kid I knew who did not smoke, did not drink beer and did not smoke pot," one of his schoolfriends, Dana James Bong, told *Seattle Times* journalist Patrick MacDonald.

But as time passed, Kurt's resolve slackened, or maybe he just learned to live with the pain, and Bong was to add, as MacDonald himself would add, that he would be doing all of those things later . . . "in excess", according to Bong; "in the ninth grade" according to Kurt.

The new amplifier made his old one look like what it had been—a real piece of shit. Kurt had never dreamed he could make so much noise, up in his bedroom for hour upon hour, blasting till the walls shook, the windows rattled, and downstairs his mother beat a frantic cantata on the living room ceiling with a broomstick.

Wendy admits that when she and Pat went shopping, they half-expected to come home and find every last piece of glass in the house shattered by the sonic attack Kurt unleashed when alone; either that, or broken by bricks from outside. The neighbors hated Kurt's guitar almost as much as she did —but not, it seems, as much as Don, during one of Kurt's visits back to his father. One day, one of the librarians at school saw Kurt walking round even more despondent than usual. His father, he said, had just smashed his guitar because he was playing too loud.

"All he had to do was ask me to turn it down," and he looked so sincere, so utterly hurt and confused, that it was possible the librarian might have believed that was all it would have taken, just a rap on the door and a "please son, but. . . ." And Kurt would dutifully turn his amp down low and apologize for disturbing him—but who was kidding who, here? There wasn't a teacher at Weatherwax High who didn't know about Kurt Cobain's stubbornness, the way he agreed to do one thing while he planned to do another, and the sheer guile with which he could make you feel guilty for catching him out when he did it.

Still, there were a few teachers who did feel some sympathy for Kurt. He was an intelligent boy—if he was bored in lessons, at least part of the reason was because he already knew what he was being told to learn. He devoured books, and when the class discussed *Rumblefish*, chances were it was Kurt who'd be asking the smartest questions—then rolling his eyes at the teacher's dumb response.

He wrote poetry, too, although that was one thing he'd never let on. It took a visit from the *Times*' Patrick MacDonald, with the information he'd gleaned from Kurt in an interview, to apprise the school's head librarian of that fact, and John Eko, MacDonald reported, seemed genuinely surprised. "That's great! I never knew that! Now maybe I can get some kids to read poetry."

Life back in Aberdeen with Wendy and Pat was essentially a repeat of life in Montesano, with one major difference. Montesano had the Melvins—the best Aberdeen could offer was Metal Church . . . and after you'd heard the Melvins, who could listen to that stuff? Kurt lapsed deeper and deeper into his own private silence, hanging out in the smokers' shed at the back of the school, staring impenetrably ahead and by his very silence daring someone to interrupt him. Very few people did.

One guy who did move into Cobain's orbit was Dale Crover—and was it coincidence or something deeper which decreed that without any intervention whatsoever from Kurt, when Mike Dillard quit the Melvins, it was Crover who replaced him? Kurt hadn't even seen the Melvins for a few months now, not since he moved back in with his mother and Pat, but now it was like he had never gone away . . . except he didn't have to go to Montesano to see them. They came to Aberdeen, moving into a spare room in Dale's parents' house, and promptly inviting all their friends down to rehearsals.

Except the band seldom rehearsed, not with an audience, anyway. Instead, everybody would be shepherded outside by Buzz, to wait on the patio while the Melvins ran through their paces. Then, every so often, the music would stop and someone would mosey by for a beer, so it wasn't a total waste of time.

Kurt was as close to the band as anyone, a number-one fan who would happily help transport their gear to shows, often wanting nothing more than his name on the guest list in return. It was the out-of-town gigs that he liked the best, in Olympia, Tacoma or Seattle—as a child, Kurt had innocently imagined that the United States was no bigger than his own backyard, and that all he needed do in search of stardom was play a few songs, and have his face on magazine covers. It was as easy as that, and as it turned out, it really *was* as easy as that. But it was those 220 mile round trips to Seattle which shaped the vision even firmer, and gave it the substance which Kurt could hang on to.

However, Kurt's attempt to join the Melvins himself was nothing short of disastrous. He had been writing songs on his own for a while now, taking pieces of his poetry and setting it to simple tunes, prompting Matt Lukin—one of the few people who heard the tapes Kurt was making—to have already earmarked him as an prodigy of sorts. It was odd, he said, "that some kid was writing his own songs, and would rather play [them] than Motley Crue!"

However, when Kurt came to audition in front of Buzz, Matt and Dale, he froze. He forgot the songs, he forgot the chords, he didn't even seem sure what the piece of wood hanging round his neck was. He just stood there, his instrument emitting howls of bored feedback, while the rest of the band waited patiently. Kurt remained their friend, but he wasn't going to be a Melvin.

He was never really going to be accepted either, outside of that circle at least. Among Kurt's other recently acquired friends was a gay guy named Myer Loftin. Their relationship, though deep, remained platonic, but that did not spare Kurt the catcalls of abuse which followed him when the other kids learned Loftin's own orientation.

Soon, Kurt grew almost resigned to being called a faggot in class, to wearily put up with the increasingly crude jokes which would echo around the changing room after gym, like "cover your butts and don't bend down," as though being gay automatically implied rampant promiscuity, and Kurt would fancy anything in a jock strap. In fact, he had almost completed High School in a state of near-total celibacy—the closest he came to losing his virginity occurred during his senior year, when he smuggled a girl named Jackie into his room. They were just about to do the deed when—the light flashed on, and Wendy stood in the doorway hissing, "get that *slut* out of here!" And the romance of the moment was lost for all time.

For a time, Kurt reveled in his presumed homosexuality; making the most of the notoriety it accrued, even if he did spend most of his time either being chased by the jocks or sat on by bullies. "I started being proud of the fact that I was gay, even though I wasn't."

However, sometimes the pressures of maintaining the facade got too much for Kurt, even though he knew that it was one of the few things in his school life which actually set him aside from the geeks and the jocks whom he hated so much. His friendship with Loftin ended, sympathetically but abruptly, because Kurt could no longer deal with the abuse it had earned him.

In later life, people around Kurt were surprised when they learned of this pre-emptory severing of a friendship Kurt clearly valued; remarked how out-of-character it was for him to so meekly bow to what can only be described as public opinion. And maybe Kurt agreed with them, and never did truly forgive himself for taking the easy way out.

Even today, homosexuality retains an absurd ability to horrify and shock people, and it's not only jerks who give the kneejerk response—one has only to look at the seething horror which emerged into daylight when President Clinton suggested allowing gays into the military. For Kurt, forever searching for new means of alienating people, the accusations that he was gay were a godsent opportunity . . . and he threw it all away.

But did he throw it away because of the way people treated him? Or because the facade in which it enfolded him was simply that—a facade. Almost exactly ten years later, Kurt would once again find himself living a lie, and in the last words he would ever write, he swore, "the worst crime I can think of would be to put people off by faking it, by pretending." In 1984, he was able to stop the game before it was too late. By 1994, he didn't think there was any way to stop it—except one. To Kurt Cobain, conformity was abhorrent. But faked unconformity was even worse.

Kurt never did lose his fascination with homosexuality, although whether it was a genuine part of his own life or simply a weapon to be used against others, he never really made clear. But the fact remains that amid his own confessions to have had homosexual affairs in the past—and his wife, Courtney Love's highly publicized claim that Kurt had made out with "half the guys in Seattle"—Kurt had no compunctions whatsoever about wearing womens' clothing on stage, nor about taking the game even further.

"I definitely feel closer to the female side of the human being than I do the male—or the American idea of what a male is supposed to be," was a typical remark; the "In Bloom" video, with Kurt decked out in full party-dress drag became a typical gesture. He gave several outspoken interviews to the gay press, and evidently encouraged his wife, Courtney, to do the same.

The first time Nirvana appeared on television's *Saturday Night Live*, in January, 1992, neatly closing a circle which began when Kurt saw the B52s in 1980, he and Nirvana's bass player, Chris Novoselic, kissed on camera. A few months before, Kurt turned up to be interviewed on MTV's heavy metal specialty show, *Headbangers Ball*, wearing a bright yellow gown. "Well, it is Headbangers *Ball*," he simpered, before berating Chris for not having given him a corsage.

Both gestures were targeted straight at the heart of uptight Aberdeen—at the same people Kurt so deliberately spited when he appeared on stage at an early Nirvana show with the back of his neck painted red. Right now, though, such brazen defiance was still some way off in the future. For now, Kurt had to simply get on with his life.

In June, 1985, he would be graduating from Weatherwax High, fading into its memory banks with barely a smudge on the walls to mark his residence there. He had yet to appear in the Weatherwax year book, and had resisted even the best-intentioned attempts to persuade him to contribute to *Ocean Breeze*, the school newspaper. There were entire courses, too, which he had blithely skipped out from, either too stoned or too bored, to do more than gracelessly flunk them. Six months before graduation, he realized that he was two years worth of credits in arrears.

He threw himself briefly into a flurry of activity. When his art teacher, Mr. Hunter, suggested that he enter some college scholarship competitions, Kurt agreed and did, in fact, win two. But his heart still wasn't in it.

Now, he whiled away his hours in blissful meditation, dreaming of how he could kill certain teachers, preferably while their sheep-like pupils watched on in horror. He had also decided that he wanted to make music his career; all that remained now was to convince his family that they'd best not interfere.

It wasn't going to be easy, though. A blazing row with Wendy, precipitated by her "slut" remark on the eve of his losing his virginity (or not), sent him hurtling for the sanctuary of a neighboring friend's house, a sojourn which ended only when his host's bewildered mother called Wendy to say, "excuse me, but I believe he's moved in with us!"

From there, Kurt moved back to Montesano, at the invitation of his step-mother. Don was less convinced that it was for the best—proud, concerned, convinced that he knew what was best for his son, the elder Mr. Cobain viewed his wife's generosity with something less than approval. But he could not turn away his own son; nor, with the boy now approaching 18, could he lay down the law in the way he might once have.

Instead, he presented just one unbreachable rule. Kurt was welcome to live with him for as long as he liked—but only if he gave up music. Perhaps he thought that would scare the boy off, and that his doorstep would never be darkened again. But more likely, he believed that Kurt would finally see sense, and when the answer came back, a shy, smiling "yes"; when Kurt dutifully trotted down to the pawn shop with his precious guitar, then came back still smiling with a small wad of cash, for a moment Don thought he'd won.

For more than a moment, in fact. A couple of days after his arrival in Montesano, Kurt took the Navy entrance examination, and passed with flying colors. Don simply glowed with pride when a recruiter dropped by the house that evening, his briefcase bulging with prospectuses, his own demeanor indicating his excitement. The gentleman didn't say as much, but Don had the distinct impression that Kurt's score was one of the highest Montesano had ever seen; one of the highest in the country. If ever a boy was cut out for a life on the ocean wave, it was young master Cobain. And Kurt sat politely, smiling and nodding. Yes, the Navy certainly did sound interesting.

The recruiter was back again the following evening.

He'd left some literature, and planted some seeds; now he wanted to see how much fruit they'd borne.

Kurt was downstairs in the basement when he arrived. His mind was wandering a little, through the exotic foreign lands which the Navy swore they'd take him to . . . the comradeship of his future fellow matelots . . . how fucking wonderfully, beautifully, brainpan-meltingly potent the joint he was smoking at that moment was . . . and wrestling. Championship wrestling. The school Championship. . . . Standing, stretching, he knew what he had to.

Back upstairs, Don and the recruiter were still talking excitedly. Yes, Kurt *was* ideal . . . well, he's had a few problems, but we got divorced, his mother and I, and he took it badly. Running with a bad crowd . . . tut tut rock'n'roll . . . all the things that parents and employers always talk about, but he's a good kid at heart, a hard worker and smart, but you can see that from his exam results can't you . . . and then a pause, as Kurt walked into the room.

"Ah, Kurt, we were just. . . . " The words hung in the air, then Kurt scythed them earthwards. "No, thanks." He turned and walked back out of the room.

Back in the basement, Kurt could hear the recruiter close the front door behind him, and Don's exasperated sigh of anger and disgust. He continued packing his stuff, and a smile danced in his eyes. When he walked out of the door, he vowed, he would never come back through it. But one thought kept coming to mind. "Good thing I never told them that my schoolmates call me faggot!"

4

Kurt was still at school when he first heard the name Frances Farmer, in 1978. A book on her life, *Shadowland*, had just been published, a Seattle-based author penning the biography of a Seattle-born actress, but there was something else there, something in the woman's eyes on the dustwrapper photograph, maybe, or even just the back cover blurb, which prompted Kurt to borrow author William Arnold's book from the High School library and begin reading.

Today, Arnold makes no bones about the fact that Farmer "obsessed" him, to the point where his own summary of the book is that it tells "the story of a reporter who falls in love with a dead woman, who looks for and finds evidence of her martyrdom, but who realizes finally that the 'truth' of her life . . . is probably unknowable."

So, Arnold wrote in April, 1994, was Kurt Cobain's. But still Arnold felt strangely linked to the tragic death of a young man he had never met, never spoken to, whose own phone calls to Arnold's desk at the Seattle *Post Intelligencer* had gone unreturned for over a year.

The day Kurt's suicide was discovered, Arnold said that the first item on his to-do list read: 'Return the call of KC—the Nirvana guy'," Arnold wrote. The note had actually been sitting there "for weeks, months even", and Arnold still cannot explain why he never returned the call, beyond the fact that his own fascination with Farmer died when the private world in which he had placed her suddenly exploded into a very public battle-ground, racked not only by lawsuits, but also "impassioned" inquiries he still received from fans.

Arnold and Cobain were not alone in their attempts to come to terms with the circumstances surrounding Farmer's tragic life; as Arnold puts it, many others, many of them troubled, saw in her story some "justification for the belief that they, too, are being persecuted for their higher qualities."

Kurt's interest, however, went deeper than most. Amidst everything else was the belief, and with it, perhaps, a lingering familial guilt, that he was somehow related to the Judge who had Farmer committed to an insane asylum, the Western State Hospital in Tacoma, in the early 1940s.

Farmer's story remains among the most horrific Hollywood has ever had to tell. Born in 1914, she was a precocious child whose personal beliefs embraced everything from nascent Feminism to outspoken Communism, and who had rattled conservative, gray Seattle society before she even left school—first with an essay in which she basically demolished the entire notion of organized religion, then by taking a trip to the USSR, funded by the local office of the Communist Party.

Farmer returned to the United States, eventually moving to Los Angeles and, in 1936, she made her film debut in a little-known movie called *Too Many Parents*. Between then and 1942, she was to make fourteen films, appearing alongside the likes of Bing Crosby and Martha Raye (*Rhythm on the Range*—1936), Walter Brennan (*Come and Get It*—1936), Cary Grant (*The Toast of New York*, 1937), Ray Milland (an adaptation of Robert Louis Stevenson's

The Ebb Tide—1937), Patrick O'Brien (*Flowing Gold*—1940) and Tyrone Power (*Son of Fury*—1942).

But even as her star rose in Hollywood, Farmer was busy making some powerful enemies. Violently outspoken, and with lesbianism added to her litany of assumed sins, she became a thorn in so many social sides that toward the end of World War Two, as William Arnold puts it, "the right-wing Seattle establishment took [her ensnarement in sundry personal problems] as an opportunity to railroad her into Western State . . . in its worst snake-pit days."

Farmer was finally released in the early 1950s, but she was but a shadow of her former self—the frontal lobotomy which medical science of the day considered to be the surest cure for mental illness saw to that. In 1958, Farmer made one final movie, flickering through *The Party Crashers*, but her career was over. She died from cancer in 1970, aged 56.

William Arnold was never in any doubt that Kurt's fascination with Farmer went considerably deeper than a simple curiosity—morbid or otherwise. "From his punkish honesty-meant-to-shock to his outbursts of violence," Arnold believed, "Cobain's behavior might be interpreted as the actions of a man determined to embody the spirit of Frances Farmer."

This conviction grew when Arnold heard the song Kurt would eventually write for Farmer—and, perhaps for himself, *In Utero*'s "Frances Farmer Will Have Her Revenge on Seattle". For most observers, critics and fans, it was simply a tribute to an actress many of them had never even heard of. But Arnold felt there was something deeper, and far, far darker lurking within the eight lines which Kurt devoted to her. "His song seemed to me a suicide note, a statement that he intended to martyr himself to avenge Farmer."

Even with the benefit of hindsight, it seems a far-fetched theory; for a writer who was scarcely even

conversant with Kurt's music to have drawn such a
deduction a full six months before Kurt's death, it
amounts to a frightening premonition. There was no
reference to Frances Farmer in Kurt's actual suicide
note, but did there need to be? Perhaps he really had
already said it once.

Kurt's teenaged interest in Frances Farmer should not
be made too much of, however. Death is a powerful
mental stimulant, particularly for people whose own
connection with the deceased is at best, intellectual—no
evidence has ever surfaced to support Kurt's supposed
belief that he and Farmer's nemesis were related, no
matter how powerfully that belief may have affected
him; and in Kurt's slowly evolving lexicon of heroes,
idols and potential role models, Farmer occupied much
the same position as Jim Morrison, Marilyn Monroe,
Marc Bolan and so on do in any other teenager's. The
tragedy of so much unfulfilled potential being snuffed
out is part of it; so is the sheer romantic potential of
Death itself. Sylvia Plath was not the darling of several
million adolescents for nothing!

Yet it is undeniable that as he approached the end of
his school career, and on into the early years of Nirvana,
Kurt's personal interests did take a remarkable turn
toward the tragic, the grotesque, even the distasteful.

He had a fascination with dolls—years later, on a
record-hunting quest which took him to a tiny antiques
shop in west London, he came across "something else
I've compulsively searched for—really old, fucked up
marionette-like wood carved dolls. Lots of them."

He admitted that he had often fantasized about "finding a ship filled with so many"—on the rocky Pacific
coast, such a ship-wrecked hoard was quite within the
realm of possibility, and besides, there is something
about the dolls which evokes the creaking hold of an
old merchantman—the legends, perhaps, that shipbound
mariners would often while away the hours of inactivity

by whittling figurines for children at home, and the wealth of sub-Gothic horror tales in which those dolls come to life. . . .

That was the sense conveyed by the apartment which Kurt and his friend, Jesse Reed, shared for a time—Kurt had already outstayed his welcome at the home of Reed's devout Born Again Christian parents; and ran through a series of low-paying, unsatisfying jobs in an attempt to keep body and soul together.

Forget the typical squalor in which two young men, living alone for the first time and lacking any concise notion of what the word housework really means, and what struck the casual visitor was the macabre tapestry of hung, drawn, quartered dolls suspended from the walls, the ceiling and the window frames, the increasingly horrific paintings of deformity and death with which Kurt decorated the walls, and a stench so appalling that one automatically (if revoltedly) scanned the dolls just in case it was one of them which was slowly rotting.

One of these visitors was Chris Novoselic, a transplanted Californian who arrived in Aberdeen with his younger brother and their Croatian-born parents in 1979.

He was instantly recognizable, a giant of a boy, taller than anybody else in school, and when Kurt was introduced to Chris and his girlfriend (and future wife) Shelli at a Melvins' rehearsal—the only place to go in Aberdeen!—the pair swiftly hit it off. When Kurt was slung out of his apartment for not paying the rent, Chris's van was one of the places Kurt called home. Another favorite haunt was beneath the North Aberdeen Bridge, a stone's throw from his mother's house.

Wendy knew of her son's plight, but had apparently convinced herself that there was nothing she could do for him. She blames her apparent carelessness on the new psychological treatment which was just coming into favor in America, the so-called Tough Love regimen.

Involving treatment which extends beyond even the implications of its name, Tough Love is an emotionally difficult program to implement, revolving around the complete severance of one's ties—financial as well as emotional—with a disruptive or violent loved one, in the hope that this will force a change in the subject's behavior. Trite as it may sound, the underlying message is sink or swim—but do it on your own.

Kurt swam . . . or at least, trod water. Indeed, the impression is that he actually enjoyed the experience, took a certain pride in the knowledge that he could survive without even a mother's love to sustain him, viewed his estrangement from all the values of his upper-working class upbringing as a genuine accomplishment.

Homeless, unemployed, often hungry, always cold, he nevertheless survived—and survived, by his own Punk standards, in style. Plus, Wendy did not completely cut him off—she would fix him lunch on occasion, and she probably knew that he was creeping into the house while she was at work, and crashing in the attic.

Kurt spent his days at the Aberdeen Public Library, sleeping, reading, and scribbling in his notebook; his evenings with Dale Crover on bass, and drummer Greg Hokanson, rehearsing those scribblings. Almost without him realizing it, he had his first band, not to mention a new place to live. He moved in with the Hokanson family, an experience which Greg's mother later described as being "like living with the devil." But she also admitted that his intelligence impressed her, while her son added, "Kurt read more books than anybody I ever knew."

He recalls renting the video of Stanley Kubrick's *A Clockwork Orange* for Kurt and him to watch one evening. The next day, [Kurt] went to the library and got the book . . . read the whole thing and then read it a couple more times, then read *everything* by Anthony Burgess." That may have been the beginning of what Kurt subsequently described as a fascination with authors whose names began with "B" . . . Burgess, Beckett, Bukowski, he'd read them all!

Fecal Matter, as Kurt dubbed his band, played a mere handful of gigs, including one opening for the Melvins at the Spot Tavern in nearby Moclips, before Hokanson was ousted and Matt Lukin co-opted to help the band record a demo tape at Aunt Mary's house. Several of the songs on that first ever demo would still be with Kurt, at least in part, when Nirvana started work on their debut album—one cut, a vocals-less dirge called "Downer", even reappeared with its original title intact.

Over the next year or so, Kurt's musical ambitions continued to keep pace with the remainder of his life—well-organized but dishevelled. He knew what he wanted to accomplish, just as he knew what the sounds were he was trying to wring from his left-handed guitar, but it was his tenacity which kept him on course, overwhelming even the vast quantities of acid he was munching his way through that first summer out of school.

A second *ad hoc* band, Brown Towel (or Brown Cow as the advertising posters misspelled it) united Kurt with both Dale and Buzz Osbourne; however, it was to be over a year before the one person with whom Kurt did want to play with, Chris Novoselic, finally contacted him to talk over the Fecal Matter tape which Kurt had given him long before. It was "pretty good"—the pair of them should start a band.

Chris's intervention was timely, to say the least. Although Kurt carried on writing and rehearsing, his continued failure to turn his music into the kind of thing he wanted to listen to was . . . not frustrating him, but at least sending him off in search of other forms of amuse-

ment. With a group of friends, he became something of
a local underground hero for the fearless displays of
offensive graffiti with which he would decorate Aberdeen, cracks like "God is Gay", "Nixon Killed Hendrix", "Abort Christ", and "Homo Sex Rules"—the
letters several feet high on the side of a downtown bank.

That was the prank which gave Kurt his first appearance in a police report. His partners-in-the-crime, Chris
and Buzz Osbourne, got away, but Kurt was taken to
the police station and told to empty his pockets. One
wonders what the desk sergeant must have made of it all
as the detritus of adolescent delinquency poured from
Kurt's trousers and coat—a can of beer, a plectrum, a
key, a mood ring . . . and a cassette by a band called
Millions of Dead Cops. That must have gone down
real well.

Kurt was handed a $180 fine (which of course he
wouldn't be able to pay), and given a 30 day suspended
sentence on a charge of vandalism; it was that experience
which encouraged him to begin picking up his life . . . if
only just a little. He landed a janitorial job at the
Aberdeen branch of the YMCA, then another as a
children's swimming instructor. Larry Smith tells a de-
lightful story of how he spotted Kurt playing with a
bunch of toddlers, leading them giggling around a patch
of garden. Nine years later, recalling his step-nephew at
the singer's memorial ceremony, Smith described him as
"the Pied Piper of Compassion".

That compassion was not particularly in evidence as
Kurt went about his daily—or rather nightly—business.
Graffiti and random acts of vandalism were accompanied
by a fairly serious bout of drug use, graduating from
acid to the codeine based Percodan and on to smack. He
didn't like cocaine, though. It made him feel too sociable.

Kurt's emotional state seemed to be worsening—even
his friends could not help but notice how he was forever
developing new nervous tics: cracking his knuckles,

twitching, the works. Aside from his music, which remained on enforced hiatus, the only thing he really seemed to care for was the tankful of turtles he installed in his latest home, a four-room shack which his mother— finally abandoning her already weakening Tough Love program—rented for him on East Second Street.

The turtles did not live much better than Kurt, although like him, they thrived. He fed them hamburger meat, changed their water when it grew too dirty, and when he was alone, or restless or bored, he would sit in front of their tank for hours, just watching them watching him, and thinking to himself—they really did have such a lot in common, Kurt and turtles. Both retreated into their shells when they felt threatened, but neither was truly safe once within. Like the turtle's shell, which is in fact highly sensitive, Kurt's own protective cocoon was no less vulnerable than what it sought to protect.

Music was his therapy. As soon as he and Chris began rehearsing together, something clicked. Kurt began widening his social circle, running down to the State capital, Olympia, to see new bands, meet new people.

He didn't like a lot of them, got bored sitting around listening to the city's self-appointed rock'n'roll spokespeople planning the revolution which would be riding into town soon on the back of international bands like Sonic Youth and Thee Mighty Caesars, the Vaselines and the Young Marble Giants, and local outfits like Beat Happening.

But he paid attention to the names they dropped, picked up the records when he found them on sale, bought *Op* fanzine (now *Option*) and read it from cover to cover, listened to the Evergreen State College station KAOS, maybe even fantasized about having a record released on the coolest of cool local record labels, K. And slowly his own manifesto began to come together.

The first band Kurt and Chris tried putting together was called the Sell-outs, a Creedence Clearwater Revival covers band, which they thought would at last bring in some steady money while they worked on more serious projects. Instead the group—which featured Chris on guitar and vocals, and Kurt on drums—broke up when bassist Steve Newman and Kurt got into a fight.

They tried again, with Kurt switching to guitar and vocals, and another friend, Aaron Burckhard, moved in on bass. Again it didn't work, although Burckhard was present when Chris and Kurt first began working out the arrangement of what would eventually become Nirvana's first single, a cover of Shocking Blue's "Love Buzz", and also at their doomed first concert together—a party in Olympia which was closed down by the police sometime before the three musicians got there.

A repertoire swiftly developed from the pages of Kurt's dog-eared notebooks—future Nirvana favorites like "Spank Thru" and "Floyd the Barber"; odd, formative things like "Aero Zeppelin"; bizarre cover versions like "Gypsies, Tramps and Thieves".

Band names, too, sprang from an unknown fertile somewhere. The trio played a few shows as Skid Row— no relation to the Heavy Metal band of the same, Skid Row was the local name for that part of Seattle where the loggers who settled the city would roll their logs down a hill to the water.

They played others as Ted Ed Fred, others still as Throat Oyster, Pen Cap Chew (which was also the title of an early song), Windowframe and Bliss—a name which would reappear on the Seattle music scene six or so years later, only to be forced out again when yet another Bliss appeared (from Toronto), and threatened dire consequences if their rivals didn't change. But finally, they reached Nirvana. Asked, years later, to define what his own interpretation of the word was, Kurt replied simply, "total peace after death."

Kurt had been evicted from his shack by now, again for not paying rent, but this time he had somewhere to go, moving in with his girlfriend Tracy Marander, at her apartment in North Pear Street, Olympia.

Like so much else in his life at the time, Kurt met Tracy during his trips down from Aberdeen. They shared a fascination with kitsch, and their tiny studio apartment soon overflowed with a combination of thrift store cast-offs, transparent anatomical kits which Kurt would painstakingly build, then fill with bizarre colored internal organs, and Kurt's own art—surreal tableaux into which he would juxtapose stories cut from tabloid newspapers; defaced religious icons; dolls, artificially aged by baking them in clay; pictures of diseased vaginas which he cut from a medical text book; and dead insects.

There is an English cartoon strip called *The Perishers*; it's been running for years, and its cast of characters is legendary in its homeland. Among them, Dirty McSquirty ranks among the most popular of all, as he wanders through the three or four frames which appear daily in the *Daily Mirror* newspaper, with a permanent cloud of flies hovering above his head.

Kurt had probably never seen Dirty McSquirty, but he was strangely proud to share the same bug-attracting attribute—particularly after he discovered the strips of fly-paper which he could suspend all over the studio, to trap and kill his six-legged visitors.

Surveying the entire scene was Chim-Chim (named after the cartoon character in *Speed Racer*), Kurt's pet plastic monkey, and a menagerie of living creatures—rats, cats, rabbits and, of course, the turtles.

Nirvana, by now, were playing fairly regularly around the North West, overcoming Burckhard's departure by recruiting Dale Crover to join them in the studio to record their first demo, with local producer Jack Endino. Of the songs they recorded, three—"Paper Cuts", "Floyd the Barber" and a new version of "Downer" (with lyrics)—actually ended up on the band's debut album, *Bleach*. Four others eventually appeared on the

Incesticide rarities collection. Kurt, who was working again as a janitor, cleaning out dentists' offices, then, unbeknownst to the dentists, taking his "bonus" in nitrous oxide, paid for the recording session.

Endino enjoyed working with Nirvana, and would remain on close terms with Chris and Kurt. "Basically," he said of Cobain, "he was just a nice guy who didn't like fame. He was not your typical rock-star exhibitionist . . . he was happy just to be making music and to get the hell out of Aberdeen!"

Copies of the tape were either mailed to, or found their own surreptitious way to every independent record label Kurt could think of—which meant Sub Pop, whose only releases to date were EPs by Green River and Soundgarden, was not included. He was barely aware they even existed! Instead, Jack Endino passed a copy of the cassette on to Bruce Pavitt—meantime, elsewhere in Seattle, Daniel House head of the C/Z label decided to offer Nirvana a place on *Teriyaki Asthma*, the first in a series of ten four song/four band 7″ EPs which he would be releasing over the next nine years.

Nirvana contributed "Mexican Seafood" to the EP, ensuring C/Z's place in history as the first label ever to release a Nirvana record, and spiraling off a piece of trivia which would return to haunt Kurt in later years.

Working on the jacket for the *Asthma* EP, designer Art Chantry and typesetter Grant Alden suddenly realized that they did not know the correct spelling of Kurt's name. They called House, only to find that he, too, wasn't sure.

"So," Alden laughs, "we just came up with the most absurd spelling we could think of." Kurt obviously liked it—the name reappeared on the jacket for Nirvana's first true single, "Love Buzz". Still, it was ironic when, years later, journalists would haul "Kurdt Kobain" out of the vinyl archive as further proof of Kurt's contrariness!

Unfortunately, C/Z might never reap their full rewards for their foresight. Working on a basis of trust and goodwill alone, House—in common, of course, with many other indie labels of the period—did not worry about contracts and the like, which meant that when "Mexican Seafood" was included on the Nirvana rarities collection *Incesticide*, he was not entitled to any share of the proceeds. He did, however, retain Nirvana's goodwill, and several years later, when House was compiling a tribute album to Kiss, Nirvana contributed what is possibly the best cut on the record, a storming version of "Do You Love Me?"

Early in 1988, Crover left the area, to relocate to San Francisco with his fellow Melvin, Buzz Osbourne; he was replaced as Nirvana's drummer by Dave Foster, but his time with Nirvana was brief. One night, Foster discovered his girlfriend was having an affair with a man from neighboring Cosmopolis, beat him up, then discovered the guy was the son of the local Mayor. Foster got two weeks in jail, was replaced by Burckhard until *he* had a run-in with the law; finally, in May, 1988, Nirvana recruited Chad Channing, drummer with a band they'd opened for back in their Bliss days, Tick-Dolly-Row.

Chad debuted with the band at the Vogue, a former downtown brothel which reputedly retains the ghosts of its bawdy past in its upper stories, and the first mixed straight/gay bar in Seattle. Although it operated only two nights a week, Tuesdays and Wednesdays, the Vogue remained one of the few club venues operating in the city at the time.

Not long afterwards, the editor of the local *Backlash* magazine, Dawn Anderson, gave Nirvana their first taste of newsprint with a short interview which prophesied, "with enough practice, Nirvana could become better than the Melvins!"

That compliment thrilled Kurt more than he could

ever have dreamed—but only until the next thrills came along. And they weren't too far away.

In the weeks since he received Nirvana's demo tape from Jack Endino, Bruce Pavitt had been to see the band play a few times. Now he wanted to know whether they would be interested in maybe doing a single for Sub Pop, suggesting gently, but firmly, that they make it that cover of "Love Buzz".

The band weren't keen—if they were going to record, they'd prefer to do one of their own songs, not some poppy little thing they only played because Chris was a Shocking Blue fan. But they relented—it was too big an opportunity to throw away on a simple matter of principle, and besides, no other labels had really shown any interest in the tape.

Plus, Sub Pop seemed keen to work with the group. They offered Nirvana five hours in the studio—during which time they recorded four songs, "Love Buzz", its eventual b-side "Big Cheese", another song called "Blandest" which was *going* to be the b-side, and "Spank Thru", which would appear in remixed form on the forthcoming *Sub Pop 200* sampler.

It was around this time, with their workload suddenly increasing, that Nirvana decided to expand its line-up by introducing a second guitarist, Hunter "Ben" Shepherd, one of Chad's former colleagues in Tick-Dolly-Row. The thought had crossed their minds before, and a number of musicians around Seattle can claim with some justification to have at least rehearsed with the nascent Nirvana, even if they didn't actually join the group.

For Shepherd, the situation was an almost complete reversal. The band was about to go out on tour, he told journalist Grant Alden, "and they just invited me to go. I was trying out for them at the time, and I knew all the new songs, but they didn't teach me any of their old songs, we didn't ever work on the old songs when I jammed with them."

Shepherd never figured out why he was asked to go along on the tour—he never played a note. the whole time he was with them! "I didn't platy at all. I was going as more like a personality check or something. It was more like I just hung out with the band, someone to have along to relieve band tension. Kinda weird, I guess—I still haven't even hashed it out with those guys why they even wanted me to go." The entire time he was with them, after all, he was busily talking himself *out* of the job. "The whole time I was telling them no way, you guys don't even need an extra guy."

Shepherd went on to join Soundgarden, replacing bassist Jason Everman at the conclusion of the band's *Louder Than Love* tour. Interestingly, however, Everman also had a stint with Nirvana, immediately after Shepherd. But his stay was somewhat longer, a period of nine months in 1989 which encompassed not only that burgeoning concert workload, but also the recording of Nirvana's debut album, *Bleach*—although he is credited as a guitarist on the record (a role he did not fulfill; the band credited him out of simple courtesy), Everman's contribution to *Bleach* was actually considerably more important. He financed the recording.

Things were moving fast, faster than anybody could ever have envisioned. And the people who knew Kurt well enough to say hello, but maybe didn't see him for more than a few hours a week, noticed something about him which they hadn't really thought about before . . . not until you mentioned it, anyway. . . . Kurt Cobain actually looked very happy.

5

The secret was—there was no secret. No secret, no hype, no word on the street which sent the sales barometer soaring the moment the album hit the racks. Looking back over the last three years, since *Nevermind* set a generation's pulse racing, a Geffen employee remembered, "we thought we'd be lucky if we sold 250,000 copies." That, after all, was where other "alternative" best-sellers bottomed out, and what were Nirvana anyway, but another alternative band, another burst of noisy rage from the latest city to sell, Seattle.

Even the band's most fervent supporters, Sonic Youth, admit that "we thought of it as another super-alluring underground masterpiece like *Bleach*, like Dinosaur Jr., that with any luck would get at least the same notoriety as Sonic Youth.

"We and Geffen thought *Nevermind* would make the selling of *Dirt* [Sonic Youth's next, Butch Vig produced, album] an easy job," Thurston Moore reflected. "Everyone in the industry said we had a gold album, but our shit's not fresh personality-wise, and there's no secret weapon as universally rocking as Cobain's voice. We were top priority at the label, but nothing too much happened. Oh well . . . maybe next time."

The first pressing of *Nevermind* amounted to a mere

50,000 copies—a mere 10,000 more than were being produced for sale in the UK! But that should still have been enough to hold things over till Christmas, at least. When the madness started within *days* of release, Geffen was forced to pull other new releases off the presses, simply to try and keep pace with the demand for Nirvana.

Before that, though, if there was any sense of excitement, it came from Britain . . . throughout the history of post-Beatles America, it always came from Britain. But usually, it was done slightly differently, usually the Brits would take something America invented, polish it up and give it an accent, then resell it Stateside and take all the credit.

They did it with the blues, and the Rolling Stones were still reaping the benefits of that one. They did it with psychedelia, and ditto Pink Floyd. They did it with sleepy singer-songwriters, and that's how we got Elton John, and, of course, they did it with Punk. (Or at least, that's what Americans like to believe.)

Grunge, though, just didn't translate into terms which British musicians could so neatly repackage. Sure the sound itself was familiar enough, distortion and muddiness, fuzz and fat bass lines; and though the term "Grunge" itself had turned up in a few happening fanzines, it certainly wasn't in widespread use in America.

But from the moment the first Sub Pop label singles went spinning out of Seattle, to land on the desk of a UK press reviewer; from the day *Melody Maker* reporter touched down at Sea-Tac airport on an expenses-paid journey to the center of the beast, then filed a delirious account of the whole "scene" in his paper, there was something so pure, so clear, so utterly unadulterated about the movement that—maybe the Brits simply couldn't improve on it, so they left it as it was, and that has precedent too, musically and geographically.

Jimi Hendrix came from Seattle, and he made his

fortune in America. But he had to go to London to make his name in between times, and when he played Monterey in June, '67, he wasn't a star, he wasn't even a speck of dry space dust. He was just some guy who'd had a couple of hits in Limey-land, who burned his guitar and played real sexy.

So it was with Grunge, although not in so many words. Few people ever called Mudhoney's *Superfuzz Bigmuff* sexy, even if it could be translated into something remarkably lewd if your knowledge of teenaged English slang was up to scratch. (It was almost disappointing to discover, later, that both Superfuzz and Big Muff were distortion pedals!)

But long before Nirvana and Pearl Jam came along, Grunge music, Grunge fashion, Grunge everything else you could think of, was already stalking the streets of London, as Bruce Pavitt, the founder of Sub Pop, proudly points out.

"Mudhoney really set the stage. . . . If *Superfuzz Bigmuff* hadn't been in the UK [alternative] charts for a year and Mudhoney hadn't been a big sensation, who knows what would have happened to Nirvana? . . . Mudhoney really opened the doors for Nirvana. . . . "

Not that Nirvana didn't work for their own slice of Britain. In March, 1989, *Melody Maker* set the stage by describing the band as "basically . . . the real thing. No rock star contrivance, no intellectual perspective, no masterplan for world domination. You're talking about four guys from rural Washington who wanna rock, who if they weren't doing this, they would be working in a supermarket or lumber yard, or fixing cars."

In truth, they probably wouldn't, but *Melody Maker*'s condescension couldn't disguise the fact that Seattle was hot, Sub Pop was hot, and Nirvana—who were at least thinking of moving to the one, and were recording for the other—were already warming their hands by the fire. *Bleach*—their forthcoming debut album—would go on to sell over 40,000 copies, and that was before *Nevermind* sent everybody out in search of it.

Nirvana played their first UK show on October 20th, 1989, in Newcastle, opening for TAD. It was alternately a magical experience—Nirvana simply didn't know so many folk in Britain cared; and a miserable journey— both bands crammed into a little Fiat van. But any headlines they won in one country, they managed to lose in another.

In Berlin, Kurt walked off stage six songs into the set, leaving his shattered guitar weeping feedback behind him. In Switzerland, Nirvana were forced to cancel a show because Kurt fell ill, and in Rome, the whole thing came close to falling apart when Kurt finally cracked beneath the strain of thirty-six shows in forty-two days, wedged into a van with ten other people, and plagued by bad sound whenever he played.

Nirvana were barely one-third of the way through their set when Kurt smashed his guitar during "Spank Thru", and went to walk away . . . here we go again. But he didn't leave the stage this time; instead he climbed a speaker stack, stood poised for a moment like he was about to dive off, then began to make his way across the room via the rafters.

By the time Kurt reached the balcony, the entire place was silent, transfixed. This wasn't part of the act, the expressions on the face of Kurt's bandmates proved that. This was somebody who was close to the edge, maybe even a few yards over it, swinging crazily through the sky, and now, on the balcony, holding a chair up over his head, and threatening to throw it onto the crowded dancefloor below.

Someone distracted his attention, someone else grabbed the chair, and Kurt was off again, heading backstage at just the wrong moment. There was an argument going on, one guy saying Kurt had broken some microphones, another one saying he hadn't.

Kurt grabbed the mikes and dropped them, stamped on them, pounded them into the hard concrete floor. "Now they're broken." Then he announced he was quitting the band, and burst into tears.

"That's how Kurt was," Chad Channing explained to writer Jo-Ann Greene. "He seemed like he was pretty capable of doing anything if he wanted to, good or bad." Even quitting the band which he had worked so hard to create.

He didn't quit, of course, and by early December he was back in London, safe and sound and ready to play. Mudhoney were over as well, and the Astoria was playing host to an event whose name had already become part of Seattle's own legacy, the Lamefest—a crop of local bands packing the biggest room they could find.

Even the billing—Mudhoney, TAD and Nirvana— was a rerun of Seattle's own Lamefest '89, held at the Moore Theater on June 9th. There, the local *Backlash* magazine complained, the sound had devastated the band. In London, Kurt had devastated his guitar collection. He was reduced to just one functioning instrument, although "functioning" is maybe too strong a word for it. Over and over, Kurt was forced to stop playing mid-song to shake the pick-up, tug on the lead, do anything to coax some sound from the reluctant guitar. But that was only the beginning.

"It all falls apart," *Melody Maker*'s post-show review insisted, "when the lanky, rubber-legged, frog-like bass-ist starts making a jerk of himself." Chris Novoselic was swinging his bass around by the strap when suddenly, something gave way and the instrument flew like a missile off-stage. "He'll have to go," *MM* tut-tutted.

Chris retrieved his instrument and the show continued. But the drama was still unfolding.

It was the Who who made a virtue from smashing their instruments, "auto-destruction", it was called at the time. Since then, it had become a religion, or at the very least, a pervasive ritual, until every new generation threw up a band whose concerts closed with the roar of splintered wood and squealing metal, and every last generation yawned. Oh, *that* old trick?

Nirvana, though, were something different. They didn't do it for show. The first time it happened, of course, it was a joke. The second time, too. But somewhere along the line the joke had stopped being funny, and Kurt used it instead to express his disgust.

Tonight at the Astoria, he was disgusted with the stop-start performance, disgusted with the way the audience had poured to the front, in spite of the show being relentless crap, and disgusted, most of all, with his guitar. As the set ended, he simply hurled it away from him, in a curve toward Chris. And Chris simply grasped his bass by its head and swung out like a batter, and that guitar just exploded into a million shrieking shards. Top *that*, Townshend!

If the American mainstream was watching these antics at all, it was from a considerable distance off from the sidelines. When Nirvana toured the U.S., it was on stages which might hold any one of a thousand hopeful no-hopers, the kind of bands who might become immense fish in their own local ponds, but who swiftly get swallowed when they make their way to the ocean.

Neither did Sub Pop have a particularly high profile at home. The Sub Pop Singles Club, the record-a-month subscription service which was launched in October, 1988 as a means of charging people in advance for a year's worth of unknown (and at the time of joining, generally unrecorded!) records was still pressing no more than a couple of thousand copies of each new release, and many of them were sent overseas.

Nirvana, coincidentally, had launched the Club with their debut "Love Buzz" single, and that kind of sums up their standing at home. They were as unknown then as any other denizen of this peculiar little club, and that includes the Afghan Whigs, L7, and Billy Childish's Headcoats, and if Seattle meant anything at all, it meant Soundgarden, the first of the city's new sentinels to land a major record deal.

Their obscurity suited Nirvana, though, and they rode their cult status for all it was worth, picking up fans and friends not because there was a buzz going on, but because they deserved them. When Nirvana played New York's Pyramid Club in early 1990, the audience included Iggy Pop, Sonic Youth's Thurston Moore and Kim Gordon, and their A&R man, Gary Gersh.

Sonic Youth's recruitment to Geffen Records in time for 1990's *Goo* album remains a pivotal moment in the history of American Alternative Rock, *not* because it represented a break with any kind of tradition—even Jane's Addiction's appearance on Warner Bros., two years previous, could not claim *that*—but because Sonic Youth themselves were pivotal, a band which reveled in revolution.

Throughout the 1980s, throughout the rise of electronic music, and sampling and digital recording techniques, a rallying cry of "back to basics" might have been expected to alienate everyone, not only because it was musically regressive, but because the basics weren't that hot in the first place. Which basics do you mean, for instance? The stuttering flame of primal rock'n'roll? The self-immolation of pulchritudinous Punk? The yammering garage roar which Billy Childish had already so perfected that even he was having difficulty getting out of Cult Hollow?

Somehow, though, Sonic Youth never ran into that problem. For starters, although a straight line drawn from the Downliners Sect to the Sex Pistols might, if you pulled it taut enough, intersect *some* of their repertoire, it was the fringes that fascinated all the way from day one.

Sonic Youth pulled out all the stops, dissonance,

distortion, destruction. At times it seemed as though
they didn't even bother playing their instruments; they
just let them feedback, then shouted to one another over
the din. But when you listened closely, it wasn't so much
that there was a tune in there somewhere, it was the
sensation that there *could* be which drew people in, and
in sufficient quantities for Geffen—until then, still tarred
as the label which brought us Guns n'Roses—not only
to draw them into the pack, but to grant them complete
creative freedom as well. And *that* was revolutionary.

Now Sonic Youth were looking for company, although
from the outside, it didn't look like Nirvana were the
kind they'd be able to keep.

The Pyramid gig was disastrous, so disastrous that
when the band got back to their motel, Chris shaved his
head in disgust. Neither was the band's debut album
Bleach, recorded before the band left for Europe, indicating anything more than average interest in Nirvana—
average, that is, for a band who could play a blinder one
night, then completely fall apart the next.

Sub Pop's own financial problems only exacerbated
the problem. By this point, the label was seriously
negotiating with various major labels, trying to fix up a
distribution deal which would ensure its releases made it
into every record store in the land, and not just those
hip enough to order new releases directly from Seattle.

Suddenly, the most immense sums of money were
being bandied about town—sums which had little to do
with the reality of Sub Pop's own negotiations and
which would, in any case, be seriously depleted by the
cost of the lawyers and advisors which the company was
suddenly having to retain.

But still, the impression was that Sub Pop were
suddenly coining it in, even before a deal had been
agreed upon, and with that perception came another;
that at last the label could afford bigger recording bud-
gets than it had previously offered. And if they couldn't,

then the aggrieved band could just pack up and go to someone else who could. It was the classic double-bind—Sub Pop needed its bigger name bands to retain the interest of the major labels, so there was no question about paying them what they thought they deserved. But by doing that, the company ran the risk of running itself straight back into the ground.

"When the [Sub Pop] book is written," Bruce Pavitt prophesied to *The Rocket*'s Grant Alden in 1992, "I'm sure it'll say something to the effect of 'Sub Pop almost went out of business, but Nirvana's *Nevermind* pulled them out.' " [Sub Pop collected percentage points from both *Nevermind* and *In Utero*.]

"Well, I'd like to clarify here and now that it was Mudhoney's *Every Good Boy Deserves Fudge*. Them allowing us to release their record [in the face of serious major label competition] really kept things going. And with or without *Nevermind*, I believe we'd still be around today."

Nevertheless, *Every Good Boy*—the album which cemented Seattle's place on the UK music scene when it made #34 on the national album chart—was still over a year distant when *Bleach* came out, and Kurt, at least, remained convinced that Sub Pop's own problems reflected badly on his album's chances. It was the same old story—turning up at gigs to find people asking where they could buy the record.

"We felt we deserved a little bit more than what we were getting," Kurt recalled in 1992, before adding what was to prove one of the most crucial remarks of his life. "I would have been comfortable playing to a thousand people. Basically our goal [was] to get up to that size of a club, to be one of the most popular alternative rock bands, like Sonic Youth."

It was that ambition, as much as the group's dissatisfaction with the way Sub Pop were handling their career, which prompted Nirvana to begin actively court-

ing major label interest. That was what Gersh was doing
at the Pyramid Club, checking out the band.

"We gave Nirvana the 'thumbs up' on both management and record label," Thurston Moore later remarked.
"We told the Geffen people we'd exert some influence
on Nirvana in good conscience."

Other labels, too, showed an interest—MCA and
Island for instance, and of course Sub Pop were still
determined to keep the group on its roster. Bruce Pavitt
and Jonathan Poneman only heard of Nirvana's inten-
tions through the grapevine, although Kurt's refusal to
return any of their telephone calls "for weeks and weeks
at a time" as Kurt later said, could have left the label in
no doubt, again in Kurt's words, that "there was definitely an uncertainty in our relationship."

It was Chris who finally broke the news to the label.
Kurt had been meant to, but when push came to shove
. . . For five hours, Pavitt and Kurt sat together in Kurt's
Olympia apartment, with the decapitated dollies staring
down at him, and the turtles clicking in the tank, discussing everything, it seemed, except the one thing that
mattered—Nirvana's immediate future.

When Pavitt went home to Seattle that evening, he
could not have been in any doubt whatsoever, but still
he had yet to hear it from the horse's mouth. When
Chris finally did acknowledge that Nirvana were leaving
the label, Pavitt later said, it was one of the most
devastating moments of his life. "I can think of very few
things that have happened . . . that have hurt my
feelings more."

For his part, Kurt, too, felt awful. He knew that the
change had been essential, that they could stick with
Sub Pop forever and never break out of their present-
day rut, or they could take their chances with a label
which had the commercial muscle to elevate them further. But that didn't stop him from regretting that things
had turned out this way, that the label which so patiently

shared his thought processes could not have shared his ambition as well.

Work on Nirvana's second Sub Pop album, in Madison WI with producer Butch Vig, essentially ground to a halt while these negotiations were underway. During just one week in April, 1990, the band recorded seven songs—"Pay to Play", "In Bloom", "Dive", "Lithium", "Sappy", "Polly" and "Imodium", named, Kurt would smile, for the diarrhea cure which Tad had been using in Europe. Rerecorded, and with "Pay to Play" retitled "Stay Away", "Imodium" renamed "Breed", these songs would become the basis of *Nevermind*—or *Sheep* as it was originally titled. Once Nirvana made their minds up to leave Sub Pop however, they simply became a demo tape.

Sub Pop were not the only casualties during these tense, but increasingly exciting, few months. Chad Channing was also on the way out, and though neither side can agree whether he jumped or was pushed, Chad admits that musically, he simply didn't see eye-to-eye with his bandmates any longer. Songs he had written for the band were being rejected—it was clear that Channing's taste for progressive rock, "elfin music" as Kurt once put it, simply wasn't gelling with Kurt and Chris' harder-edged pop tastes.

It didn't help, either, that Kurt had spent so many years playing drums. He was a terrible back seat driver.

A British tour scheduled for March, 1990, was cancelled, but Nirvana did not drop out of view. Dale Crover moved in to the vacant drum seat for the week-long West Coast tour which Sonic Youth had invited Nirvana along to support.

Dan Peters of Mudhoney then took over, and the band returned to the studio to record what would become the b-side of their penultimate Sub Pop single, the maniacal "Sliver", and for a show at the Motor Sports International and Garage on September 22nd—a show, incidentally, which spawned some of the best-known photographs of Nirvana ever published. One, by Sub Pop's regular photographer, Charles Peterson, even graced the Seattle *Rocket*'s first issue following Kurt Cobain's death.

The final change in Nirvana's hitherto tempestuous line-up was wrought later that same evening. Dave Grohl had known Buzz and the Melvins for some time now, ever since the Aberdeen band hit Washington DC on one of their periodic tours. He'd met Kurt and Chris as well, although neither he nor, thankfully, they, remembered too much of the incident when Buzz finally reintroduced them.

Grohl's then-current band, the DC hardcore group Scream, were in Olympia for a show, and afterwards, they piled down to a party which they'd heard was the hottest thing happening in town.

Maybe it was, but Scream weren't impressed—particularly when some girl plugged in her electric guitar and started playing her songs, "total bad teen suicide awful music," as Dave put it later. Dave retaliated by running out to the car and grabbing a Primus tape. What he didn't know, and wouldn't until he repeated the story to Kurt and Chris later, was that the girl was Tobi, Kurt's latest girlfriend.

Dave arrived in Seattle to meet Kurt and Chris on the evening of the Motor Sports gig. According to legend, he arrived at Sea-Tac airport with his drum kit in a cardboard box, his clothes in a stuffed plastic bag, and an apple, which he promptly offered to Kurt.

The singer looked at the fruit in dismay. "No thanks. It'll make my teeth bleed." Inwardly, Dave groaned. He'd barely spoken twice to Kurt, and both times he'd put his foot in his mouth.

Despite his now somewhat checkered past with the band members, however, Dave was a natural for Nirvana, slotting instantly into Kurt and Chris' already established hegemony and even—during the sessions for

In Utero—getting one of his own songs down on tape!
"Marigold" ultimately appeared on the b-side of the
"Heart-Shaped Box" single alone, but producer Steve
Albini spoke for many people when he remarked, "of all
the 'pop songs' we recorded, 'Marigold' was an obvious
stand-out."

Kurt added his own public seal of approval to Dave's
recruitment by describing him as "the drummer of our
dreams." Privately, he went even further, inviting Dave
to share his apartment, and volunteering his couch as the
drummer's own sleeping quarters. What did it matter
that the couch was a full foot shorter than Dave, and
he'd be sharing the room with Kurt's pet turtles? For
Kurt at least, rooming with Dave was to be a lesson in
socialization, and his friends unanimously agree, the
singer was definitely coming out of his shell. Maybe the
symbiosis which they'd conjured between Kurt and his
beloved amphibians wasn't so permanent as they thought
it had been?

In other ways, too, Dave's arrival at the Olympia
apartment was fortuitous, if not downright therapeutic.
Kurt and Tobi, she of the "total bad teen suicide awful
music," broke up shortly after Dave arrived in Seattle,
and for a time, the singer lapsed into absolute silence,
self-absorbed to the point of morbidity.

"We would sit in his tiny, shoe-box apartment for
eight hours at a time, without saying a word," Dave later
laughed. "For weeks and weeks this happened." Finally
the pair were driving home from rehearsal one evening,
when Kurt suddenly chirped up, "You know, I'm not
always like this!" "And I just went 'Whewww'."

Things moved swiftly over the next few months.
Dave's first show with Nirvana, in Olympia, just weeks
after he joined the group, sold out within a day of tickets
going on sale—something Grohl had never experienced
before. A management contract was in the offing, pairing
Nirvana with their friends Sonic Youth under the aus-

pices of Gold Mountain, in L.A. The search for a new label, too, was heating up, from both sides of the counter. Nirvana were keen to get on with their second album; and half the music industry, it seemed, was keen to put it out.

What was happening to Nirvana, of course, was no different to what was being experienced by many other Alternative, and in their wake, pseudo-alternative bands. MTV had locked into the heart of what was clearly shaping up to be a grassroots movement, devoting two late night hours a week to *120 Minutes*, a showcase for alternative videos.

The Red Hot Chili Peppers, an outrageous L.A. funk rock band, had just chalked up a major hit single, after five years spent kicking ass on the club scene. Faith No More and Jane's Addiction were on the verge of earning their first gold records. Depeche Mode, New Order and the Cure had each graduated onto the stadium circuit. There was no corroborative evidence, but it suddenly looked as though America was getting heartily sick of the pristine, prattling pop which had financed the music industry throughout half of the '80s, and was finally getting back into something with a little more . . . integrity? Meaning? Energy? Guts? It didn't matter what the word really was—Nirvana, and all the countless other bands who were out there on the same circuit, had it. All that remained for them now was to make sure they could put it where it needed to be.

That was one side of the coin. The other side, and Kurt apparently spent a week very seriously considering it from every angle he could, was that simply signing on the dotted line could make very rich men out of him and his bandmates. After that, they could do what they liked . . . and that included breaking up the band.

It was an audacious, if not particularly novel idea. Fifteen years before, the Sex Pistols had recklessly swung their way into infamy simply by signing a record

Kurt Cobain
1967 — 1994
A Tribute

(AP/Wide World Photos)

Cobain's fans paid their silent respects in the park next to his home. (Photo by Curt Doughty)

The "garage" of the home belonging to the Nirvana frontman, where his body was found by an electrician on April 8, 1994. Seattle police reported cause of death as an apparent self-inflicted gunshot wound. (Photo by Curt Doughty)

Friends crossed the police line to visit with family the day after news of the tragedy broke. (Photo by Curt Doughty)

Cobain's body was removed from his house and taken to a medical examiner's van on Friday morning. (AP/Wide World Photos)

(Left:) Throughout the day, fans left flowers and lit candles outside the home. Security guards protected the family and property. (Photo by Curt Doughty)

(Below:) More memorial flowers at the entrance of Kurt Cobain's home on Saturday morning. The note reads "We love you, we'll miss you. Meg, Elisa, and Shira." (AP/Wide World Photos)

MTV scrapped its usual pre-taped format when the news was announced, and went on the air with live coverage, interviews, and tributes all weekend. Tabitha Soren provided updates from the scene. (Photo by Curt Doughty)

Cobain's death cast a pall over SubPop Records' annual party (planned for Saturday April 9). The bash turned into a wake the day after the tragedy was discovered. A media blitz arrived at Seattle's famous Crocodile Café to obtain any comment. (Photos by Curt Doughty)

Mourning fans burned candles and said quiet prayers at Sunday's Seattle Center memorial. (Photo by Curt Doughty)

Reverend Stephen Towles addressed the crowd at the Seattle memorial for Kurt Cobain. (Photo by Curt Doughty)

Marco Collins and other local alternative DJs shared their memories. (Photo by Curt Doughty)

Kids, fans, and friends began gathering at the Seattle Center in the early morning for the vigil. Over 4,500 people eventually arrived. (Photo by Curt Doughty)

The memorial on Sunday was sponsored by three local radio stations. (Photo by Curt Doughty)

On Saturday night in Cobain's original hometown, Aberdeen, Washington, about 300 fans held a candlelight vigil at a waterfront park to remember the city's most famous native. (AP/Wide World Photos)

deal, then getting tossed off the label . . . signing a second one, and getting fired again. They came out of it with something in the region of a quarter of a million dollars.

Now here were Nirvana being offered *four times* that much simply for signing with one label! And if they split up when they'd cash the checks, Kurt mused, who'd be able to stop them? Oh, the lawyers could wrangle and wring their hands in despair, but at the end of the day. . . . it *was* a tempting idea.

But so was that of seeing just how far Nirvana could go under their own steam, and though the deal they eventually signed, with Geffen, was less than those they'd been offered elsewhere—$287,000, compared to the cool million which Capitol Records apparently dangled—at the end of the day, Nirvana still came out on top.

"We have one of the best contracts any band has ever had," Kurt boasted. "We have complete control over what we do [a legacy of Sonic Youth's own demands when they signed to Geffen], and what we release, which literally means that if we handed in a 60 minute tape of us defecating, [Geffen] would have to release and promote it."

For now, however, he would be content simply to get *Nevermind* out of the way. Resisting Geffen's attempts to pair the band with a "big name" producer—R.E.M.'s Scott Litt and Neil Young's David Briggs were both mooted by the label—Nirvana would continue to work with Butch Vig, even though he had never produced a major label album before. Neither, Nirvana responded, had they.

Work on the record, which would include rere-cordings of several of the songs intended for the second Sub Pop album, got under way in May, 1991, in Van Nuys, CA. The budget, $650,000, was almost precisely one thousand times larger than Sub Pop had given them for their first record, and while that had only been a single . . . what was an album anyway, if not half a dozen singles?

When Kurt thought in those terms, however, he wasn't thinking purely in terms of music and money. Like so many other people who grew up during the 1970s, who watched, even from afar, the starburst of Punk at the end of the decade, the single was still the medium which most suited rock'n'roll, a one-off roar which captured an essence; the sound of a band, but its message, its very *zeitgeist*.

The Pistols' *Never Mind the Bollocks* was a great album, but it never recaptured the magic of "Anarchy in the UK". The Clash made a killer debut, but "White Riot" said as much in three minutes as *The Clash* said in more than thirty. That had even been the thinking, too, behind the Sub Pop singles club—new bands, new sounds, and none of them took more than four minutes to listen to. As Kurt joined Vig and the band in sorting through the songs which would make the album, that was the idea at the back of his mind. If I heard this song on the radio, what would it tell me about the people who made it?

"Territorial Pissings", "In Bloom", "Lithium", "Breed", "On A Plain", "Come As You Are", "Something in the Way"—as the sessions rolled on, and the album took shape, somehow the whole thing seemed flawless. Was there a weak moment in earshot? "Albums this good aren't only hard to find," raved *Alternative Press*' review, " . . . they're scary!"—which was an impetuous way of explaining something which was on a lot of people's minds just then, the fact that every so often, an album appears which simply defies all expectations, which is just *so* good, so perfect, that it seems impossible to believe that the studio itself wasn't imbibed with its magic, and that the engineers standing around the control room, the gophers, the people passing by on the street outside, weren't magically drawn into its orbit, so that when it was over and the music had stopped, they would walk away dazed, lost, but stunned by the majesty of what they'd just witnessed.

Nevermind was one of those albums, and no, the magic wasn't immediately apparent. Chris even admitted that the first few times he heard "Smells Like Teen Spirit", even while he was recording it, it never struck him as anything out of the ordinary.

Not until he heard the play-back did he concede that, hey, that song "really rocks;" and even then, he had no idea just what he'd been part of creating. No one did, from the band to their label, to the workers at the pressing plant who would pull a switch then blankly watch as the black 45s or the silver CDs plopped from the press, and moved off to be bagged.

But from the moment the first copies of the song were serviced to American radio, on August 27th, 1991, it was clear that something was afoot. In Seattle, its release coincided almost precisely with the launch of a new alternative radio station, KNDD, affectionately known as The End not only for its call letters, but also because it fell at the end of the dial, 107.7 FM, and almost from the beginning, the station took to airing "Teen Spirit", a new song for a new station.

WOZQ, broadcasting out of Smith College in New England, once spun the record 67 times in a single week, including once on a reggae show!

MTV swiftly joined in the fun, debuting the "Teen Spirit" video with a much trumpeted World Premiere on *120 Minutes*, then in October, slipping it into the Buzz Bin. Sources at Geffen claim that *Nevermind*, almost a month old by that time, was already on the verge of going gold before MTV began airing the video with any regularity, and that MTV simply served as a "multiplier", adding extra sales to an already burgeoning bandwagon.

What that calm analysis fails to consider is the sheer
nationwide impact of MTV, the fact that it infiltrates
communities which might not even have an alternative
radio station, and certainly don't have alternative record
stores. "Smells Like Teen Spirit", it was later decreed,
was important because it cut across all the generic
boundaries which rock'n'roll in the '90s has erected
within itself.

That is true, but it did it *not* because everybody was
secretly awaiting the new Nirvana album—most people
still hadn't even heard of the band the first time they
heard the song. It did it because it was *allowed* to cross
those boundaries, and in crossing them, blur them.
You'd hear "Teen Spirit" on alternative radio, but you'd
hear it on the Metal stations too, and the Hard Rock and
all the others which recognized what Kurt himself had
recognized six months before.

It's not great albums which make the difference, it's
great *singles*. And up there with "Anarchy" and "Hound
Dog", "Metal Guru" and "Rock and Roll parts one and
two", "Smells Like Teen Spirit" was a great single.
"When [it] comes screaming from the local radio, nothing
else sounds so right all day," said *Alternative Press*, and
that kind of hit the nail on the head—"Savage pop
stranded so far out on the edge that the slightest push
could propel it into legend."

The song lent itself to so many different applications
that it was difficult to know where to start! Early on in
the single's career, MTV sent their cameras out on the
streets to ask people if they had a clue what the song's
lyrics were. Some folk got some parts, others got others,
but basically, no one had a clue. The comedian Weird
Al Yankovich even made a record about the confusion,
recounting the melody line which was now burned into
pop culture, but asking, "the lyric sheet's so hard to find,
what are the words, oh never mind. . . ."

It wasn't only the fans who were confused, either.

In her book *Route 666 On The Road to Nirvana*, Gina Arnold—by then a fairly long-time Nirvana associate—wrote, "when I heard that *Nevermind*, an album whose first line [from "Teen Spirit"] is 'Load up on drugs and kill your friends", had gone to #1 . . . my first thought was '[President] Bush will not be re-elected'." One wonders what she would have thought if she'd known what the real lyric was . . . "load up on *guns* and *bring* your friends." It actually sounds more like an incitement to vote Republican.

Nevermind hit the top of the chart in late December, 1991, pushing Michael Jackson's *Dangerous* from its #1 perch in the very same week as Nirvana themselves joined the Red Hot Chili Peppers' latest tour, second on the bill. They were only booked for a handful of shows, which would conclude with a New Year's Eve show at San Francisco's Cow Palace. From there, Nirvana would move on to the Pacific Northwest on their own, to headline their own festive concerts.

But the time they shared the stage with the Peppers, sandwiched between the funk-mugging headliners and the hard rock density of bill-openers Pearl Jam, was enough not only to cement their own sudden impact, but also that of Alternative Music in general. In the home of the Grateful Dead, in a city whose New Year's Eve was traditionally surrendered to Deadheads alone, 15,000+ kids throwing off the shackles of a past which most of them were too young to even remember, but had been hidebound in service to anyway, were celebrating *their* music in *their* own way.

That was the night that Nirvana's painstakingly auto-destructive set ended with the band deliberately un-screwing every nut on their instruments to hasten their imminent destruction. A few reviewers, and maybe some fans as well, felt cheated afterwards, which might be why Nirvana did it. Not because they were scared of looking stupid, slamming unyielding guitar into unbuckling amp, but because it simply *wasn't the way things are meant to be done*. In the three months since "Teen Spirit", nothing about Nirvana had been done the way that it should be.

The next three years would prove no different.

6

Kurt had always talked a big fight. One former Sub Pop employee vividly remembers him asking when the label was going to make him a star, and toward the end of 1990, he was telling the UK music paper *Sounds*, "All my life, my dream has been to be a big rock star." He had even figured out how he was going to do it.

His new songs, he maintained, the ones which would eventually surface on *Nevermind*, were far more pop-oriented than their counterparts on *Bleach*—he'd even coined a phrase which would soon be emblazoned across Nirvana's latest press kit, ". . . the Bay City Rollers being molested by Black Flag. . . ." "We figure . . . ," Kurt continued, "we may as well get on the radio and try and make a little bit of money at it."

Now, suddenly, they couldn't get *off* the radio, and had made more than a little money. Geffen's investment in the band at the time of the album's release amounted to little more than $550,000. Within four months of its release, *Nevermind* had sold over three million copies in the U.S. alone. One Geffen rep was even heard boasting that he hadn't had to spend his promotional budget yet. "People are coming to me, now!"

Pop historians were swift to dig into the archives and unearth other occasions when lightning struck gold—

Bruce Springsteen in 1975, Peter Frampton that same year. . . . The difference was, both Bruce and Frampers had considerable careers behind them, and had already done the legwork which in a perfect world (as theirs' apparently were) *would* pay multi-platinum dividends. They had toured their butts off and made the right friends.

Nirvana were different. True, they had toured incessantly; since completing work on *Nevermind*, they barely left the road for a moment—from American clubs to European festivals, then back to the American clubs, and only when their sales took off did they start to see the insides of anything bigger.

But in 1975, America was desperately seeking a new rock messiah, someone who would have the impact of a Dylan, the charm of a Beatle, the conviction of a Stone. Arguably, both Springsteen and Frampton each matched two out of three, and the course of their subsequent careers ultimately decided which criteria were the most important. Springsteen was elevated to Godhood, Frampton made one not-so-hot album, and he disappeared overnight.

The early 1990s, however, made none of the demands on its idols that past generations had been forced to endure. Suddenly, superstar was simply a job, with all the ups and downs of any other, and just as you wouldn't pursue a plumber for his autograph, simply because he did a good job unblocking your sink, why would you chase a musician because he'd just played a good show?

"When I got into Punk Rock, the attitude was 'kill all the rock stars'," Dave Grohl told *Alternative Press (158)*. "And autographs are something the whole Punk thing was against." Now, Nirvana were signing so many that Kurt joked about having a rubber stamp made up, with the word Autograph on it. He'd never dreamed of getting Evel Knievel's autograph when he was a kid— why would anyone want his? Again, this was the 1990s!

But the Star Machine which had once made such a fuss about its produce wasn't really dead, was it? Rather, it was just lying fallow, starved of attention, starved of new product, because Stars, real superstars, are never just the boy next door, the girl in class, some normal Joe with a T-shirt and a gee-tar, no matter how hard the PR tries to kid the kids otherwise.

They're not manufactured, though, either, and a million shattered careers can prove that, lying belly-up by the side of the road with their dead dreams in tatters all around them. "I could have been a contender . . ." I thought I was a contender—that's a crock of crap, just like when Kurt would go into Sub Pop and tell them to make him a star.

Because he didn't want to be a star, he just wanted to make a living at his job, which is all most people ever really want to do. They dream of being God and snorting the national debt up their nose every night, and if that was all there was to it, then all would be fine. But really, that's just the beginning, because in a way, being a true Star really is like being God, and that's a burden which very few people could ever, would ever, want to have to shoulder. Not really. And Kurt Cobain least of all.

Alternative Press put it best. "In September, 1991, Nirvana was just a local cult, the latest alternative morsel to drop down Geffen's gullet. By October, they were U2 and Springsteen, Presley and the Pistols, rolled into one snarling bundle." And if that had been their musical brief, the standards their admirers expected them to maintain and live up to, then maybe all would have been well.

They weren't, though. Because suddenly, Nirvana weren't just Bono and Bruce, they were Roseanne and Oprah as well; they were the three-headed baby which was found on the moon, and Elvis is working at a K-Mart in Kansas; they were a cure for cancer and a cause of common cold, they were everything that screams out BUY ME on the supermarket check-out line.

"A lot of people look at us and wonder what we're complaining about," Dave remarked in June, 1993, as Nirvana girded up for the launch of their third album. " 'Money, fame, groupies, the world at your feet . . . I wouldn't have any problems with that!'

"What they don't understand, what they'll never understand unless it happens to them, is the way it changed *everything* overnight." Later in that same interview he would muse that Nirvana was essentially the end of his life. "I could be 43 and an English teacher, and I'd still be Nirvana's drummer."

Kurt echoed his thoughts, casting his mind back to the days on either side of *Nevermind* and saying, "it was like I went to bed one evening, and everything was fine, but when I woke up the next morning, they said on the news that I was an escaped Nazi child killer." And the first he knew about it was when the firebombs started landing on the bedspread.

"Of course we reacted badly!"

His response was in stark contrast to the remarks he'd made the previous April, when Nirvana adorned the cover of *Rolling Stone* for the first time. Answering queries about how he was dealing with his new found, but scarcely-sought fame, Kurt replied, "it really isn't affecting me as much as it seems . . . in interviews, and the way that a lot of journalists have portrayed my attitude. I'm pretty relaxed with it."

People who knew him told a different story, however, and theirs' were the ones that passed into the widest circulation. Nils Bernstein, today publicist at Sub Pop, opined, "People are treating him like a God and that pisses him off. They're giving Kurt this elevated sense of importance that he feels he doesn't . . . deserve. [He] is ready to strangle the next person who takes his picture."

Kurt continued to demur. He did concede that "I think we've almost gotten too big . . .", but the crux of his statement appeared to be the word "almost", as though he still wouldn't mind clambering a few more rungs up the ladder first. "Every waking moment of my life is Nirvana now. . . ."

And while it was true that he was finding it harder "to work up the energy to go into the audience to watch the opening act, because everyone asks for autographs", even that task was gradually becoming easier. "I'm learning to deal with it now."

But was he? Again in the words of *Alternative Press*, "Todd Rundgren coined the phrase, but Kurt Cobain has made it his own: the Ever-Popular Tortured Artist Effect. He courted fame not by words but by being, and not until it was too late did he learn just how many age-old equations he fulfilled."

AP's October, 1993, profile of Nirvana was slammed in some corners for being overly sensitive towards Cobain, as though the band's very reputation for contrariness and difficulty was itself sufficient for hatchet-job journalism. In truth, it was an attempt to portray the group *without* all that baggage, to simply corner them in a Seattle Broadway restaurant and let them lead the conversation. It seemed to work as well.

"Personally," the writer penned, "I found [Cobain] immensely likable, but the qualities I admire in a person are not necessarily the right ones for America's first Punk superstar. Not unless they can be 'revised' somewhat.

"So his natural shyness has been translated as indifference; his modesty as paranoia; his honesty, arrogance; his intelligence, pretension. And when a San Francisco journalist clocked those pin-prick pupils and skin so sallow it defied definition . . . oh look, mommy, we've got another junkie pop star to play with."

The first public reference to Kurt's drug use did indeed appear in San Francisco, in the January, 1992, issue of *BAM* magazine. The singer was "nodding off in mid-sentence," and his physical symptoms suggested "something more serious than mere fatigue."

A couple of months later, *Hits* magazine reported that Kurt had been seen "slam dancing with Mr Brownstone"—"Guns n'Roses slang for heroin", as *Rolling Stone* helpfully explained shortly after.

Kurt flew to his own defense, telling *Rolling Stone* that not only was he *not* doing heroin, "I don't even drink any more because it destroys my stomach. My body wouldn't allow me to take drugs if I wanted to, because I'm so weak all the time." Besides, he continued, "drugs are a waste of time. They destroy your memory and your self-respect and everything else that goes along with your self-esteem. They're no good at all." He didn't deny that he'd tried them, of course, but "in my experience, I've found they're a total waste of time."

If that was the case, Kurt had been wasting a colossal amount of time. According to Michael Azerrad, author of *Come As You Are*, Kurt returned to smack for the first time since his pre-Nirvana days in November, 1990. It didn't impress him. "It sucked, it's stupid. It makes you feel gross and bad. I just wanted to try it." Maybe it was the expression on Dave Grohl's face which did it, but Kurt sounded genuinely contrite when he continued, "don't worry, I won't do it again."

In actual fact, he was doing it about once a week, for the hell of it as much as anything else, but also, he told his ex-girlfriend Tracy, because it made him feel sociable. Once, with cocaine, that had been a problem. Now, with stardom, it was a necessity.

Kurt did his best to keep his drug use secret, and for a long time, he succeeded. It was only when Chris started noticing the same people, or the same type of people, in Kurt's company, that he realized that things were getting beyond the simple experimental stage.

"I run into [Chris] backstage at gigs sometimes, and

he pretends he doesn't know me, or doesn't want to know me," Kurt revealed once. "It's like 'Oh shit, the junkie; if we don't look his way, he may be too stoned to see him.'" The fact that he rattled off this diatribe in front of a Geffen press officer maybe diluted its truth just a little, but there was no doubting the fact Chris, like Dave, disapproved strongly of Kurt's escalating habit.

For a time, it even looked as though it could cause an irreparable breach in the band. Chris is the first to admit that for a time, he, too, had a problem—with drink, rather than drugs. But he overcame it, and having done so, it was hard to see why Kurt was not doing the same with his problem.

It was not, after all, as though Kurt had been doing heroin all his life—only since *Nevermind* turned the band members' entire world upside down had he been seeking solace in anything outside of the usual post-teen amusements. But the band was slowly getting a handle on its new-found status, and as it did so, the pressures lessened . . . or at least, they would if only Kurt would stop creating new ones to take their place.

At the same time, though, Kurt was writing some of the best lyrics of his life, and while neither he—nor, mercifully, any of the pocketbook pop psychologists out there—ever credited heroin with forging a Lennon-on-acid-like renaissance in his writing talents, the question does arise.

At what point did Kurt stop writing things like "Floyd the Barber", and come up with "Teen Spirit" instead? Of *Nevermind*'s mightiest moments, both "Teen Spirit" and "Come As You Are" post-date Kurt's first taste of smack and if, as its fiercest opponents all reckon, there's nothing like smack for dulling the senses, as Kurt had found, it also dulled inhibition and shyness.

By his own admission, for the first time he was writing songs which actually talked about how he felt—*Bleach*, he said, had nothing to do with his own emotions, and even now, "I very rarely write about one theme or one subject. I end up getting bored with that theme and write something else halfway through the rest of the song, and finish the song with a different idea."

But "Teen Spirit" at least touched a nerve in a lot of people, whether it was the confusion inherent in the words you can't singalong to (or at least, couldn't; nine months after the album came out, the lyrics were printed on the "Lithium" CD single sleeve), or the passion in the tone, or simply, as Butch Vig later said, "I don't exactly know what 'Teen Spirit' means, but you know it means *something*, and it's as intense as hell."

That intensity was what heroin reawakened in Kurt; that, and a welcome relief from the near-constant agony of the arsenal of ailments to which he was by now all but martyred—the stomach pains which still left him doubled up, and which a succession of doctors had proscribed to a succession of complaints; the back problems which had dogged him on and off for years, and which, in the guise of minor scoliosis, caused curvature of the spine; the weak chest which always reminded him how prone he was to bronchitis; and a pharmacist's utopia of sidebar syndromes, most of which were down to his own attempts to subvert the original problems.

"[Kurt did have] a kind of self-destructive streak about him," Chad Channing told journalist Jo-Ann Greene. "He kind of brutalized himself in weird situations, he could get down on himself very easily, especially during the early days." But most of what Chad witnessed, he says, was down to Kurt's ill-health. "We were touring and what-not, and he was always fighting whatever his stomach problem was, and bronchitis and other things, getting really upset with it. Literally, he'd just take a stick and start beating himself in the chest, just hoping he could loosen some of the [phlegm] . . . 'ah, man, fuck this!' "

Doctors, Kurt himself once said, "simply want to take

my money and stick their fingers up my ass." Heroin
dealers wanted his money just as much, but at least they
offered some solace. By late November, 1991, only a
couple of months after they first started going out together, Kurt was introducing Courtney Love to his
hobby in Amsterdam . . . not, as was later so salaciously
reported, *vice versa*. "*I* was the one that instigated it,"
Kurt insisted. "It was *my* idea."

Later, following the couple's return from Europe, they
lost their first home together, sharing an apartment
with Hole guitarist Eric Erlandson, because he wouldn't
tolerate their habit, and for the next few months, home
for the Cobains was a string of four star hotel rooms.

The Red Hot Chili Peppers' tour at the end of 1991
probably marked the lowest point in the rest of Nirvana's
own battle to come to terms with Kurt's drug use—
although his actual performance did not seem to have
been impaired by his habit, his physique clearly had
been. Some nights, Kurt looked dead, others he looked
as though he'd passed beyond even that stage, and was
now working in hideous zombie overdrive, and those
people privy to his secret were amazed not that he
continued to function so well, but that he was able to
function at all.

It was that, more than anything, which kept the
rumor-mongers as quiet as they were—sure Kurt looked
like shit, but until *BAM* finally came out and called a
spade at least a shovel, there was nothing to prove that
he was doing it too.

Later, of course, it seemed as though everyone had
known what was going on, and the stories piled up like
snowdrifts at Christmas—tales of Kurt shooting prior to
Nirvana's appearance on *Saturday Night Live* on January
11, 1992, and throwing up afterwards were common
currency for a long time. So were the reports from
various amateur AJ Webermans, rifling through the Cobains' trash following their relocation to an apartment on

Spaulding Ave, in L.A.'s Fairfax district, and coming up with nothing but cigarette-burned blankets—a sure sign that *someone* was nodding out nightly. And so was the claim that Kurt even turned up at his own wedding strung out.

It is surprisingly easy to glamorize drug use, not only to oneself (or those one loves), but also to the public at large. The subject is one of those which lies at the heart of the seemingly (and tiresomely) eternal battle between the rock/pop establishment and those moral and religious groups which would, to paraphrase the immortal words of the British band Carter USM, burn us *all* at the stake "for playing punk rock." In 1984, the brothers Dan and Steve Peters, of the fervently anti-rock music oriented Zion Christian Center, summed up their own feelings on the subject by warning, "the devil is most free to toy with our minds when they are the most relaxed"—and of course, you don't get much more relaxed than when you're stoned out of your head! "Rock, drugs and death—somehow they seem forever entwined."

Gary Hermann, author of *Rock & Roll Babylon*, was flying under similar, if more secular, colors when he opined, "once upon a time, drugs were seen as a route to a new form of musical expression. Today . . . drug-taking in quantity is all too often seen as the reward and proof of rock stardom. And between taking drugs to make music, and making music to take drugs, the performers, the music and the fans have lost more than the law could ever take."

Even Kurt admitted that his habit wasn't quite as romantic as it might seem from afar. The constant references to his addiction in the press, veiled though many of them apparently were, were getting to him. He was spending more and more time worrying that the police were about to burst in through his front door (or whichever front door he was calling his at the time—the hotels were still the nearest thing to home), slam him up against the wall in search of the track marks which were becoming increasingly pronounced, and cart him off to jail. There, he was certain, he would simply be left to rot through withdrawal, and he'd probably end up dead. "That was kind of scary."

Yet still rock's chroniclers guiltlessly recite the litany of sainted rock martyrs, and attribute their brilliance as much as their deaths to their habits.

Jimi Hendrix used to drop 300 micrograms of acid before every show, and if he did things with the guitar that other people had never seen done before, it was because he was experiencing things they'd never experienced before. Popular legend insists that Johnny Thunders never went onstage straight. Beach Boy Dennis Wilson talked openly of his own use of drugs throughout the period while the band were making their most influential album, the legendary *Smile*. And Janis Joplin once summed up her ambitions by admitting, "all my life I just wanted to . . . get stoned, get laid, have a good time." Or, live fast, die young, and leave a great looking corpse.

Kurt wasn't stupid. He was well aware that he was walking a very tentative tightrope; that unless the authorities actually legitimized drug use, regulated the sources and forced the filth from the business, every shot could be the one which sent him hurtling into oblivion—he was a Sex Pistols fan, he'd read what happened to Sid Vicious, celebrating his release from Rykers Island with his first shot in two months, completely unaware that the smack he was shooting was 90% pure. He knew the dangers, and he knew that they outweighed the benefits.

But he also became very good at denial—not in the psychological sense which was bandied around following his death, that he really had succumbed to the junkie delusions of invulnerability, but in the sense of maintaining the appearance of health and efficiency. "I have

never been fucked up in front of a journalist!" he told
Alternative Press in 1993, a year after he assured *Rolling Stone* readers that drugs were a complete waste of time.

The writer on that occasion was Michael Azerrad, and though he was convinced that "it was pretty obvious the guy had a monkey on his back", he dutifully reported Cobain's words with neither contradiction nor complaint. Months later, having been recruited to author the band's own biography, he asked Kurt why he lied.

Kurt's answer highlighted an aspect of his personality which in many ways sums up the awful conflicts which his new found role as an (albeit unwilling) "spokesman for a generation" had foisted upon his shoulders. "I had a responsibility. I had a responsibility to the kids not to let on that I did drugs." It was difficult, even frightening for him to accept, but "it just so happens that there's a bunch of people that are concerned with what I have to say." The problem was, "I'm just as confused as most people. I don't have the answers for anything."

It is also telling that Kurt, when he wanted to, was quite capable of simply dropping the dope from his diet for days, even weeks.

Maybe that's what made him so increasingly unpredictable, the fact that nobody ever knew for sure whether he was on anything or not; nor, once even he acknowledged that he was addicted, whether his own attempts to wean himself off the drug would work. Throughout Courtney's pregnancy, he made sure that he only shot up when she was elsewhere; or, if she didn't leave the house, somewhere she wouldn't see him.

He then dropped the habit completely when Nirvana set out for a summer, 1992, tour which took in a series of increasingly prestigious festivals, including a headline slot at England's annual Reading show—a genuine mudbath whose thick brown residue still stains the garments of anyone foolish enough to get too close to the mosh pit.

Throughout his time abroad, Kurt remained clean,

replacing what was fast becoming a $400 a day heroin habit with a methadone substitute which at least kept the craving away; before that, while his wife lay in one wing of the Cedars-Sinai hospital in Los Angeles, suffering the pains of labor, Kurt was in another, undergoing the equally excruciating horror of withdrawal. What was it Grace Slick once said—"it's hard to keep an eye on the kid while you're hallucinating"? Kurt wanted to be clean when his daughter was born, and when *Vanity Fair* published its accusations about baby Frances' parents, he could genuinely turn to the world, clean and healthy. He even rode out the shock waves of a *Los Angeles Weekly* story, in January, 1993, documenting Courtney's stay at Cedars-Sinai hospital.

Less than nine months later, however, he was back on the drug, and on May 2nd, 1993, he arrived back at the couple's home near the North Seattle waterfront from a party, shaking, delirious, flushed. Some $30 to $40 worth of smack were coursing through his veins, although it wasn't immediately clear that he was overdosing.

On the police report, Courtney states that she thought he was suffering from cotton fever, brought on when fibers from whatever was used to filter the smack, cotton, or a cigarette filter, found its way into Kurt's bloodstream.

According to Courtney, it wasn't the first time this had happened, but this time was worse, a lot worse. With Kurt's mother and sister Kim looking on, Courtney gave her weakening husband a shot of buprenorphine, a stimulant which, while illegal, is recognized within the medical profession as having a reviving affect on both cotton fever cases and heroin overdose casualties. She also fed him a fistful of pills—four codeine based Tylenols, three Benadryls and a Valium, to try and induce vomiting.

It didn't work—nothing worked. Finally, she called

for assistance. Kurt was rushed to Harborview Medical Center on 9th Ave. That time he was lucky.

The following month, the police were back, this time in response to noise complaints. Courtney had stumbled upon a cache of guns which Kurt had hidden around the house—guns, in the same house as an already inquisitive nine-month-old child.

The couple began fighting; then, according to a report in *Q* magazine, fought again when the officers, having already scooped up a number of firearms (including several of those which would be returned to Kurt shortly before his March 18th altercation with Courtney) reminded them that under local law, "one or other of those involved in domestic disputes must be carted away [to jail]. Kurt loses, and spends the next three hours in custody before being released without charge."

What amazed people was the fact that the couple were battling now to decide which one of them should take the rap!

Throughout the summer of 1993, Kurt's drug use was never far from the surface. Nirvana's interview with *Alternative Press* was disrupted for over half an hour when Kurt, having already sat down in the restaurant and ordered his meal, suddenly announced that he had to go out for a moment. By the time he returned, his chicken was cold, Chris had vanished, and Dave was talking happily about his love of antique clocks.

"Where's Chris?"

The press officer charged with presiding over what was looking like an increasingly ill-starred interview sighed. "Home."

"Why?"

"He was waiting for you and. . . ."

"And he thought I wouldn't be back, 'fucking Cobain the junkie, pissing off to score.' " Actually, Kurt explained with a patience which his flashing eyes clearly belied, he'd been to visit his chiropractor. "I was feeling like shit, I needed to relax, I had a fucking massage. And even if I hadn't, what business is it of his? Have I ever missed a show, or missed an interview, or not done anything I said I would do, because of anything else?"

The question was open-ended, but Kurt didn't really expect an answer—not because his record was fairly spotless, but because the real point of his question, the fact that he had never allowed drugs to impair his performance, was so rhetorical that it defied any response whatsoever.

Whether he had missed shows, or simply messed them up, was immaterial. The fact was, Kurt's behavior was fast reaching the point of no return, although it would take another nine months, and another frenzied bout of touring, before anybody realized just how fast it really was traveling. For now, he was still able and willing to put a brave face on it all.

"We don't have the right to complain [about our success]," he smiled. "We all decided to do this. And we could decide to end this any day."

7

They looked, said *Sassy*, very *Sid and Nancy*, reference to the mid-'80s cult movie detailing the last days of Punk icon Sid Vicious and his girlfriend, Nancy Spungen.

It was a none too tactful observation. Notorious junkies, succubus and incubus, their story ended when Sid OD-ed in February, 1979, two months after he was arrested and jailed on a murder charge. Nancy had been found stabbed to death in the couple's New York Chelsea Hotel room the previous October. Since then, a glamor which Sid had never known during his short, 21-year, life had attached itself to him; had spread to encompass his romance with 20-year-old Spungen; had essentially cast the pair as a Punk Romeo and Juliet, living their own doomed love to its logical, ghastly conclusion.

For Kurt and Courtney, however, the parallels were not so strained. They were indeed junkies, were indeed notorious, and when they checked into hotels, it was as Mr. and Mrs. Simon Ritchie—Vicious' real name.

Did the connection end there, though? Sometimes, it seemed hard to believe that it did. Right up until his death, Kurt maintained that it was purely coincidental that he met the two most important influences of the last years of his life—Courtney and Heroin—all but simultaneously, towards the end of 1991. He continued to insist that it was he who encouraged Courtney to take the drug in the first place and not, as some people seemed to assume, the other way around. He even admitted that she was so squeamish about needles that very often, he'd have to inject the drug into her himself. Otherwise, he reckoned, she'd have never got it together.

Love was the archetypal Punk, albeit a decidedly well-travelled one. She was born in San Francicso on July 9, 1965, the oldest child in a family which eventually grew to encompass five half-brothers, five half-sisters. Today, she says, they all "have masters degrees, and went to college from the day they were born."

Her mother was the psychologist Linda Carroll, herself no stranger to the headlines following her professional involvement with the fugitive murderer Katherine Anne Power; her father, Hank Harrison, authored a Grateful Dead biography, *The Dead: A Social History of the Haight-Ashbury Experience*. He hung out with that band as well, and in 1969, his four-year-old daughter was included in the friends and family photo on the third Dead album, *Aoxomoxoa*.

The family moved to Eugene, Oregon, and Courtney moved tentatively into show business—inspired, she reckons, by seeing Tatum O'Neal win an Oscar for *Paper Moon*. "I owned the Pacific Northwest when it came to the children's slot in radio jingles and voice-overs." But while Courtney was still young, her parents broke up, and she moved out to New Zealand with her mother. Mom lived in a commune, Courtney was packed off to boarding school. When she was ten, she was transferred to another school in England, when she was 12 it was back to Eugene, to stay with her mother's therapist.

Her mother remarried, and by the early 1980s, Courtney and her new family were living in nearby Portland. It was there that she was placed on parole on a shoplifting rap—parole she promptly violated when she ran away from home. When she reappeared, she was hauled off to the first in a long succession of local juvenile care facilities and foster homes.

She spent some time in Liverpool, England, hanging out on the explosive music scene which had already produced talents of the stature of Dead or Alive, Wah!, Echo and The Bunnymen and Teardrop Explodes. Then, in 1983, now aged 18, Courtney took her first well-paying job, working in a local drag queen disco; the following year, she was in Minneapolis, forming Sugar Baby Doll with Kat Bjelland and Jennifer Finch, future founders of Babes in Toyland and L7 respectively.

The band, she later shuddered, was "an awful lot like Lush, very girly vocals and all that. I just hope no tapes of it ever get out."

"All through my teens I moved from scene to scene," she once commented of this period, but the only thing it taught her was that there is no scene there. "It's like a desert." From the outside, people would look in and wonder—hey, what must it be like in *that* city, *there*, hanging out with stars, living the music, but once you're in there it don't mean jackshit, and it's only in retrospect that everything congeals in your own mind and an essence seems tangible." Which was just as well anyway, because as Courtney added, "I'm almost too loud and too opinionated for a scene."

In San Francisco, she sang briefly with what would become Faith No More, as they took their first tentative steps into the limelight, and enjoyed a short stint with Social Distortion. Briefly, she was married. And in Alaska, she was so broke that she took a job as a stripper, and spent the next few months working her way down the West Coast, saving her cents in every new town she undressed in. "I was earning $200 a night as a Sunday Girl, when the tit-job girls had the day off, and were saving up for guitars."

Finally reaching L.A. (but still stripping for a living, at Jumbo's Clown Room), she tried her hand at acting

for a while, coming to the attention of director Alex
Cox, and in 1987, taking one of the lead roles in his pop-
spaghetti-western *Straight to Hell*. Before that, though,
she auditioned for the female lead another of Cox's
movies—*Sid and Nancy*.

She lost out in the end to Chloe Webb, and instead
turns up only briefly toward the end of the film, as one
of Nancy's grieving friends. Five years later, while the
rest of the world was damning Cox for not exercising
more prescient judgement, Courtney at least was relieved that her "big break" had broken before it got
going. "Can you imagine . . . ?"

"It looked like I could be a nice little actress," she
reminisced. "[But then] I thought, 'who wants fame for
fame's sake? How desperate do you have to be to go on
Oprah or Donahue and talk about how you fucked your
four year old kid'?"

In March, 1990, Courtney formed the band which she
still leads today, Hole, and fell straight into a ready-
made pigeonhole, the "Foxcore" scene which Thurston
Moore jokingly conjured up for them, L7 and Babes
in Toyland.

And it didn't even matter that Hole were not an all-
female band, that guitarist Eric Erlandson—recruited
after he answered an ad Courtney placed in the L.A.
magazine *Recycler*—stood out "like a dick at a hen party"
as one writer crudely remarked, because the focus of the
band was Courtney all the way . . . the first time Kurt
Cobain saw her, she reminded him of Nancy Spungen,
but was it the blonde hair which did it? Or the way she
always seemed to say what she thought, often without
stopping to think if it was a good thing to think in the
first place.

Courtney's introduction to the Nirvana camp came via
Jennifer Finch, who in turn was friends with Dave
Grohl. What happened next was straight out of a high
school romance—Courtney told Dave that she fancied

Kurt, he told her that Kurt liked her back, and she gave him a present to hand to the singer, a red heart-shaped box, decorated with flowers and filled with pine cones and sea-shells, a doll and doll's tea set. Kurt never said thank you, but he hung on to the gift—later, it would become the center-piece not only of a song, but also the picture sleeve of the first single from *In Utero*.

Months passed, and their paths never crossed. Then, in May, 1991, they arrived independently at a Butthole Surfers gig at the L.A. Palladium. Courtney spotted Kurt first, walked over and thumped him in the stomach. He returned the blow—and things just went on from there. Instead of goodbye, Courtney bade a fond fare-well with a swift kick.

"There's this thing called groupie radar," says a girl who claims she ought to know; "groupies can spot a rising star from a mile off, long before anybody who's paid to see such things can do it. The trouble is, that means you only know that it works in hindsight. When Courtney first started hanging out with Kurt, it was—so what? Nobody thought he would amount to anything. It was only afterwards, when Nirvana made it, that people went 'ah, the old radar's still going.' "

Courtney admits that she hung around older groupies at one time. But it was back in the early '80s, and she wasn't that good at it. "I was intrigued . . . but I wasn't pretty enough. I had no style or tits." And besides, in the months before *Nevermind* was released . . . before it was even recorded, the best will in the world could not have placed Kurt's star higher than Courtney's. She later revealed that when they first discussed marriage, she demanded Kurt sign a pre-nuptial agreement . . . to make sure that *he* couldn't run off with *her* money!

Hole's first album, *Pretty on the Inside*, had smashed into the UK independent charts, and Courtney's love-me-or-despise-me-*with-a-passion* persona had won even more hearts among the UK rock press than any Seattle grunge monster ever seemed likely to.

"Years ago in a certain town," Courtney mused early in 1994, "my reputation had gotten so bad that every time I went to a party, I was expected to burn the place down and knock out every window. So I would go into social situations and try my best to be really graceful and quiet and aloof"—qualities which *Spin*'s Dennis Cooper, studying her "hellishly beautiful punk-derived image," suggested might be closer to the real Ms. Love than she was willing to let on. "But sometimes when people are bearing down on you so hard, and want you to behave in a certain way, you just do it because you know you can."

Rumors of her temper became legendary, around Seattle and spreading like ripples, throughout the entire music industry. A long-running battle with post-Goth rockers Shadow Project continued to fester long after the band itself had shattered—according to guitarist Eva O, "Courtney was mad because she thought I stole Hole's bass player [Jill Emery] away for Shadow Project. Maybe she forgot that Jill and I were working together for a long time [as the sadly-missed Superheroines] before she joined Hole."

Calvin Johnson, head of the Olympia-based K Records, was apparently on the receiving end of a Courtney blow one night—and that despite her husband proudly sporting a home-made K logo tattoo on one arm. Victoria Clarke, author of an as yet unpublished, unauthorized Nirvana biography, allegedly felt the weight of another; and one night in a Seattle 7–11, a young Nirvana fan called her "Courtney Whore", and she ended up getting a fistful as well. According to Courtney, there was a lot more to those tales, but she didn't want to go into it. "Everyone likes to gossip about me," Courtney smiles. She revealed she had hooked her computer up to the

America Online network, simply so she could punch her name in, "and there'll be all this crazy stuff about me."

In fact, there were crazy stories everywhere—particularly where Kurt was concerned. Among the miles of footage shot for Sonic Youth's *1991: The Year That Punk Broke* movie, is a scene from the 1991 Reading Festival, Nirvana slotted midway through the first afternoon, just before Chapterhouse, while Kat Bjelland, Kim Gordon (of the Pixies) and Courtney sit backstage when a camera popped round the door. Courtney looks deep into the soul of the camera and says, "Kurt Cobain makes my heart stop. But he's a shit." Then she leaves the room.

What made this particular incident seem so retrospectively poignant was the fact that at the time, throughout the first months of her friendship with Kurt, Courtney was still going out with Billy Corgan, frontman with Chicago's swiftly rising Smashing Pumpkins. Like Nirvana, they had recently completed a studio date with Butch Vig; but while *Nevermind* still hung round the starting blocks, *Gish* was up-and-at-'em, a blistering potpourri of '90s Punk and '70s rock, slammed through a grinder purely of Corgan's own invention.

"[Courtney] . . . had a profound effect on my writing and my music," Corgan told *Alternative Press*. "If she had her act together, she could obscure someone like Patti Smith—she has that much raw talent. And in terms of intelligence, almost a genius in an insane kind of way." But, he gloomily predicted, "she'll never get her due because she's a cartoon character in a way."

It was in the aftermath of the *Vanity Fair* story which came so close to shattering Kurt and Courtney's lives that he continued, "she's completely wound up in the whole idea of rock'n'roll, the mythology, making sure everyone thinks you're cool, shooting drugs . . ."

According to Corgan, Courtney was on her way to visit him when she flew out to Chicago on October 12, 1991. Nirvana were in town the same night, playing a show at the Cabaret Metro, but until Corgan, in his own words, "flipped out [and] made her leave my apartment," she had no real intention of going to see them. Now, though, she went to the show, or at least to the party thrown at the end, and again according to Corgan, "she gets completely fucked up, goes home with Kurt, fucks Kurt, calls me the next morning and begs me to let her come back to my house. That's the way it happened."

Which is somewhat more prosaic than a rumor which, when it was related to Kurt, even prompted him to recoil in bemused disgust - that she sashayed up to him at the party, and they had sex at the bar while everybody watched. In reality, the closest they came to consummating a relationship which they both now knew was fated to happen was a kiss, a wrestle, and an impromptu cross-dressing session for Kurt. When she tumbled from Corgan's apartment, Courtney had gathered up at least some of her luggage, a bagful of lingerie which so fascinated Kurt that he ended up putting it on.

Courtney became a regular sight as Nirvana's fall 1991 U.S. tour rattled on, and again in Europe, where Hole's continental tour was following a similar course to Kurt's—similar, but not precise. Courtney cancelled at least one show simply so she could travel to Amsterdam and spend some more time with Kurt. And like Chris and Dave, her own bandmates could do little more than watch while the lovebirds canoodled.

There was something almost alarmingly compulsive about the relationship, there always is when two people this intense come together, in love or in war, or in anything else. Abrasive to the point of near-self-destruction, they apparently thrived on random abuse. Flashing back to the party in Chicago, somewhere between the kiss and the fashion show, the couple had a riotous time throwing glasses at one another.

Courtney called it a "mating ritual for dysfunctional people," and Kurt admitted that half the fun of being in public with her was the knowledge that at any moment, someone could leap out and attack her with a knife—simply because "she seems . . . the kind of person that attracts things like that." She retaliated by calling him "a big piggy grump." She knew, as so many of Kurt's friends knew, that he was not always like that.

Kurt had another agenda as well, however, the knowledge that the rest of the band, the rest of the Nirvana entourage come to that, would have real problems relating to the knowledge that Courtney was there to stay. He could already see the scenario unfold before him, like the scenes in *Spinal Tap*, where Derek Smalls' girlfriend takes over the reins, or the nightmare visions hashed out of a thousand Beatles bios, Yoko Ono in pointy hat and long black cape, casting her *avant-garde* magic over a defenseless John Lennon, " . . . the bitch who's ruining Nirvana . . ." she deadpanned, but though she could smile when she said it, it hurt.

But Derek Smalls only got what he wanted, Lennon just took what he needed. And sticking with fact over Hollywood fiction, the Ono comparisons had further credence as well. When the King of the Moptops described "Don't Worry Kyoko", anything from four to fourteen minutes of bleating feedback bleeding into squealing Yoko, as "one of the greatest rock'n'roll records ever made," sure he was being contrary, but he was also speaking the truth as he saw it.

Courtney, forever, it seemed, on Kurt's arm or his coat-tails, popping up in his press like a wild-eyed, shrieking Jack-in-a-box, fit the role model like a glove, then clasped it to her bosom. The news that the couple intended marrying, delivered to the band less than a month before Courtney discovered she was pregnant by Kurt, only compounded her image. They would do the deed on February 24, in Waikiki, right at the end of Nirvana's Far Eastern tour.

Surely, though, there were some other issues to be

sorted out first? Kurt was still heavily into smack; the general assumption, naturally, was that Courtney was as well. According to Kurt, though, even at its height, her habit was scarcely worth mentioning, and the moment she discovered she was pregnant, Courtney stopped using altogether. A short time afterwards, the couple consulted a specialist in birth defects, who assured them that so long as the withdrawal wasn't too bad (and in Courntey's case, it wasn't), a woman could continue using smack during her first trimester without serious harm befalling the baby.

However, there is a vast gulf between recognized medical opinion, and knee-jerk public reaction, particularly when drugs and babies are concerned. Even Chris and his wife Shelli were infuriated that the couple could even consider allowing the child to be born under the assumed circumstances, a rift that resulted in the Novoselics being conspicuously missing from the upcoming wedding.

The ceremony was held on a beach-side cliff top, Kurt wearing green pajamas, Courtney a lace dress which had once belonged to the actress, Frances Farmer. There were only a handful of guests in attendance—Dave Grohl, Kurt's guitar tech Nick Close, the band's sound engineer, Ian Beveridge, their tour manager, Alex MacLeod, best man and long time friend Dylan Carlson, and his girlfriend.

It was a brief, and not altogether joyous occasion—Chris's absence in particular cast a shroud over the entire proceedings, but deep down, Kurt appears to have respected his bass player's stance. Just as he himself had a right to convictions which sometimes overrode even his own friends' best wishes, so he acknowledged that others, too, had the power to make their own decisions and stand by them. It was all part of being a spokesman for a generation, he supposed.

* * *

For Kurt and Courtney—and logically, Nirvana as well—much of 1992 was devoured by preparing for the baby's arrival, although the group was seldom absent from the pop limelight.

In March, Tori Amos released the first of what would later become a cottage industry of lightweight Nirvana covers, a version of "Smells Like Teen Spirit" which Kurt promptly, but not unkindly, labeled "a great breakfast cereal version."

There was also a tape moving into underground circulation in Seattle of Sara deBell performing the same song in pure Muzak fashion—the Muzak Corporation, of course, has its headquarters in Seattle; had, in fact, at one time or another employed many of the people who would later come together to create what would be called the Seattle Sound, Sub Pop founder Bruce Pavitt included. *Grunge Lite* was finally released by the local C/Z label in 1993.

These early tributes to Nirvana, to the rapidly accumulating body of evidence pointing toward Kurt's songwriting genius, were as unexpected as they were welcome, although when the band was rocked by a dispute over the fair division of publishing royalties, also in March, they could only have served to further disturb some already turbulent waters.

Having initiated a straight three-way split between the band members back in the days of *Bleach*, Kurt was now demanding a 75% share of royalties which was more in line with his actual, physical, contribution to Nirvana's repertoire. Dave and Chris agreed it was a fair move—even without his own name attached to the individual songs, Kurt was already widely known as Nirvana's chief songwriter, with all the pressure and persecution that role could entice.

What rankled was his demand, six months after *Nevermind* appeared, that the new arrangements be applied retroactively—a request which essentially meant that

Kurt's bandmates would not see another penny from
Nevermind until he had finished collecting his due. In
extreme circumstances, were it possible for *Nevermind* to
stop selling as swiftly as it started, it could even leave
them in substantial debt to Kurt.

Their attempts to reason with Cobain, however, came
to naught. For a week, phones were slammed down
upon one other, and Kurt was even considering quitting
the band, unable, he complained, to believe that his
bandmates were being "so greedy". That, it appears,
was when Chris and Dave gave in. Kurt got his money—
now all that remained to be seen was whether it would
make him any happier than he was. Or any luckier.

As the year progressed, it seemed that the answer to
both questions was a resounding "no".

In July, with Nirvana away in Europe playing a
rescheduled string of Irish and Scandinavian dates which
they had cancelled back before Christmas (plus further
shows in France and Spain), "Lithium", the third single
from *Nevermind*, was released in July, its cover art including a still from the sonogram Courtney had just recently
undergone. Just as the doctors had forecast, and the
Cobains angrily insisted, the baby was fine—even if
Kurt did insist she looked like a kidney bean. Courtney
agreed, and the baby already had half of her name.

But once again, the gulf between medical and public
opinion is vast and hazy, and the European tour—
coming on top of the royalty squabble—saw Nirvana
almost literally lurching from crisis to crisis.

Kurt was off heroin, sublimating his cravings with a
methadone substitute; Courtney, six months pregnant
and reportedly delighting in displaying every mood
change to which her hormones took a fancy, was clean
as well. But who would believe a story like that, especially when Kurt was rushed to hospital in Belfast, on
June 23rd, suffering from . . . what?

Gold Mountain put out the story that he'd eaten too

much junk food, and was suffering from a bleeding ulcer. Kurt himself reckoned he'd forgotten to take his methadone after the previous night's show, and was now suffering so much from his stomach that all he wanted was to be taken away and pumped full of morphine. And someone else decided that he'd OD-ed on heroin, and called the British tabloids to let them in on the drama.

Gold Mountain promptly hired a pair of bodyguards, with instructions not to let Kurt and Courtney out of their sight. Unfortunately, they should also have added that Kurt and Courtney ought not know they were there—and certainly told them not to simply sit outside their hotel room, waiting for the couple to get up in the morning.

Kurt was onto his shadow in a moment, and the moment their back was turned ("even minders have to use the bathroom!", one observer smirked), he and Courtney hustled their possessions together and fled the hotel. They checked into another, and for 24 hours they remained wilfully, gleefully *incommunicado*, just sitting around imagining the furor which would have erupted the moment their absence was discovered.

Aside from the Nirvana entourage's misgivings about Courtney's influence upon her husband's behavior (which had in any case been deteriorating the longer the tour went on), there were also some very real fears about her condition.

No one doubted—although they never could prove—that life on the road was hardly the most conducive for a six months pregnant young woman, and when the tour reached Spain, it seemed as though their worst fears were about to be justified.

Courtney suffered contractions—mild, as it transpired, compared to the true pains of imminent childbirth, but sufficient to convince her that something was going terribly wrong with her pregnancy. Even worse,

Nirvana were about to step out on stage when the emergency occurred.

For a few awful minutes, Kurt was undecided—should he play the show, and hope for the best? Or drop everything and accompany his wife to the hospital? He chose the former course, but the moment the concert was over, he was racing to Courtney's side.

It turned out to be a false alarm, but just to be on the safe side, the couple's L.A. obstretician counselled the couple to return home immediately. They followed his advice, and walked straight into another calamity.

Operating his own vision of home security, Kurt had hit upon the idea of storing his most valuable possessions—his guitar, some notebooks, and some tapes—in the bath tub. "No-one would ever think of looking there!" he chuckled proudly. "There's not a burglar in the world who'd think of robbing a bath-tub."

He may well have been right on that score. What he hadn't reckoned with was the state of the plumbing in their Fairfax apartment. During their absence, several gallons of foul-smelling sludge had apparently exploded out of the plug hole, overflowing the bath as a matter of course, and destroying Kurt's books, tapes and guitar.

Neither was it Kurt alone who was being stricken by this appalling run of misfortune. "We've been hit with the most amazing shit," Grohl told *Alternative Press* a year later. "And nearly all of it is lies." The rest, it appeared, was simply opportunistic greed.

Towards the end of the 1960s, a duo emerged from Britain's psychedelic underground bearing the name Nirvana. They weren't bad, in a dippy, dreamy, multi-instrumentalist way, and as the decade dripped towards its demise, the band—Patrick Campbell Lyons and Alex Spyropoulos—released five albums, some singles, and one minor hit . . . "Rainbow Chaser" kissed the Top 40 in May, 1968.

By 1972, the band had run its course, and while

Campbell-Lyons briefly revived the name in 1976, 1978 and 1981, even a well-received 1987 compilation of their mid-period work hardly sent people scurrying into the streets to spraypaint their name on the walls of the world. A full *two years* into the American Nirvana's chart-topping career, however, these ghosts from a long distant past re-emerged, arguing the same kind of case as has historically proven the bugbear of so many English bands in America—it's our name, and you're wrecking it.

(Strangely, Nirvana were not the first band of that name to have emerged with fangs bared in the months since *Nevermind*—a Christian band of the same name had lodged a complaint back at the end of 1992, after a show they staged in Los Angeles was invaded by an enormous crowd of kids demanding to hear "Teen Spirit". The northwestern Nirvana eventually purchased their southwestern rivals' copyright on the name.)

The case never came to court—according to Dave Grohl, it was easier to pay up than make their adversaries prove their point in court. "When all this is over," Grohl growled, "I'm going to become a lawyer."

All this, however, paled when compared to the storm clouds which were now gathering, unforeseen if not wholly unexpected, on the horizon, ready to break on the very eve of baby Bean's scheduled birth.

With all the benefits of hindsight, one can wonder precisely what Courtney thought *Vanity Fair* magazine wanted with her. True, she was a musician, and one with a fair bit of notoriety behind her. It was also true that Geffen had just united her and Kurt on their own artistic roster, paying a reported $1 million for Hole's signature. That was worth some press coverage in itself.

But *Vanity Fair* is not known for its in-depth coverage of music industry business affairs; neither was the interviewer, Lynn Hirschberg, widely regarded as one of the Fourth Estate's softer touches. At best, as Courtney later admitted, the ensuing article would further embellish her anti-establishment reputation. And at worst? It is very unlikely whether Courtney, Geffen, Gold Mountain or anybody else connected with the couple could have ever conceived of that. Although maybe they should have?

At what point did Hirschberg's profile of Courtney Cobain become, in the author's own mind, a platform for indignant moral rectitude? Before the interview, when Courtney was still simply little more than a figment of scandalous imagination?

Or later, during Hirschberg's background research, when she suddenly found herself seemingly inundated by industry insiders (all of them unnamed) who "fear[ed] for the health of the [unborn] child?" When she noticed that despite her advanced pregnancy, Courtney still smoked cigarettes? Or when Courtney made the statement which would appear in print as an outright admission that she had continued using heroin for "a couple of months" after she discovered she was pregnant?

Hirschberg's reporting was criticized for its misinterpretation and misinformation. Sympathizing with Courtney's plight, several writers painstakingly highlighted a number of very basic factual errors in the story, mainly names, dates and places.

Others drew upon their own experiences with Courtney, remarking upon her own propensity for sarcasm and humor, then questioning the construction Hirschberg seemed to place upon a remark like, "if there ever is a time that a person *should* be on drugs, it's when they're pregnant, because it sucks." But that all came after the fact.

Hirschberg's article appeared in *Vanity Fair*'s September issue, hitting the stands just two weeks before the baby was due. Courtney checked immediately into the hospital, simply to escape the media circus which was already exploding around her; Kurt followed her, drawing upon inner strengths which even he wasn't certain he possessed, and cleaning up, to paraphrase Courtney, at perhaps the only *other* time when a person should be on drugs—when their entire world has just fallen apart.

In the outside world, the piranhas were going bananas. Their prey was down, they could smell the blood, but those damned hospital doors were unyielding. Public opinion, however, was not. Suddenly it seemed that everywhere you turned, every mention of Courtney, Kurt and their unborn child, was accompanied by horrifying photographs of crippled crack babies, and calls not only for the baby to be removed from its parents the moment it was born, but for those parents to be removed from society. People who did not know the couple, who may, until this blew up, have lived their entire lives in absolute ignorance of their very existence, were suddenly calling for their heads on a platter.

That certainly seemed to be what happened at the Los Angeles County Department of Children's Services, whose case against Kurt and Courtney seemed to revolve around Hirschberg's revelations, and a urine test which dated back to a test Courtney took early on in her first trimester. The evidence was scanty, and the Cobains' lawyer fought hard, but it impressed the Family Court. Just before Frances was born, the court ordered that Kurt undergo another thirty days' detox.

Frances Bean Cobain was born at 7:48 A.M. on August 18th, 1992. According to legend, as soon as Courtney went into labor, she climbed out of bed and, with her IV trailing behind her, crossed the hospital to Kurt's room, and screamed at him to get out of bed. "You are not leaving me to do this by myself, fuck you!" Scarcely aware of what on earth was going on, Kurt followed her back to the delivery room, then threw up and passed out just as the baby began to be born.

She was named after Frances McKee, of the Vaselines—had she been a boy, she would have been called after another of the group, Eugene Kelly. It was only later, following the release of Nirvana's third album, that people began associating her name with that of the actress Frances Farmer. It would certainly have been appropriate.

At the beginning of September, Kurt and Courtney reappeared before the Family Court. Still no final decision had been rendered in the case; until one was, Frances was placed in the care of one of Courtney's sisters, Jamie. For the next month, Kurt and Courtney were legally prohibited from being left alone with their own child.

It was a heartbreaking period, but one which the couple had to get through. They certainly couldn't expect any assistance from elsewhere.

"One of the reasons we signed with Geffen," Kurt reminisced later, "was because we believe in what David Geffen stands for, which is a very left-wing, very caring, very honest outlook. He's said that at his age [he was 49 in 1993], he doesn't even know what Alternative Music is. But his whole outlook is Alternative.

"The downside of that is that he doesn't have the muscle to protect his artists in the same way as, say, certain East Coast labels with underworld connections."

At the height of the tabloid feeding frenzy which the *Vanity Fair* story unleashed, Kurt contacted his label head to see if some screws could be tightened, if the lies could be quashed. "I found David didn't do things that way. We just had to weather the storm"—weather it, and watch while his band's public profile slipped even deeper into the abyss . . . and Kurt himself plunged even further than that.

At some level in their minds, the Cobains knew they ought to take some comfort from the knowledge that it often proves very difficult indeed to have a child removed even temporarily from its parent's custody. The bonds of natural parenthood are so strong, and so important, that even the Law, that proverbial ass, thinks twice before trying to sunder them.

But as they mourned the estrangement of their new-born daughter, Kurt and Courtney were not looking for comfort, nor were they really expecting it. It is often said, usually by the disadvantaged underclasses who watch as their better-off peers get away with figurative murder, that there is one law for the rich, another for the poor. So there sometimes is, but if the question had been put to the Cobains in September, 1992, there is no doubting which side of the fence they would have come down upon.

They were being treated like this *because* they were rich, or at least, because they were famous. It was late '60s England revisited, the forces of law, order, and obeisance to an unspecified common good descending like the wrath of God on the Beatles, on the Stones, on any long-haired pop star who dared question the way things had *always* been done, and maybe put forward suggestions about how they could be improved.

It was ridiculous, but the authorities were even has-sling people for wearing the band's T-shirts—a Geffen employee using an L.A. cash machine was actually told by the police to turn his Nirvana T inside-out because it was offending passers-by! All it said was "Crack smokin' kitty pettin' flower sniffin' baby kissin' corporate rock whores."

No, even more than that, it was Frances Farmer all over again, only this wasn't 1930s Seattle, it was 1990s L.A.—which just went to prove that society never really changes, it just updates its weaponry every once in a while.

"I used to be an extremely negative person," Cobain acknowledged. "My attitudes and opinions have only got more optimistic in the last couple of years, and that's because of having a child and being in love. It's the only thing I feel I've been blessed with. That's the life I want.

For years, that's the life I was searching for. I wanted a partner, I wanted security, I wanted a family." And now this. "I can't decide whether I like playing music enough to put up with the shit that's written about us, especially the shit that's written about somebody I totally love."

In the midst of all this, Nirvana were due back in England to headline the Reading Festival—more than that, to take their place at the head of an afternoon line-up which had been personally selected by Kurt, and did indeed read like a tribute to his own musical fascinations.

From the northwest, the Screaming Trees, Mudhoney and the Melvins. L7 were there, and were instantly rewarded when their latest single, "Pretend That We're Dead", breached the UK chart. Eugenius, the near-eponymous band put together by former Vaseline Eugene Kelly, made the billing; so did Pavement, Nick Cave and, deferring to Nirvana's penchant for blasting Abba's *Greatest Hits* album through their tour bus when they traveled, the tribute group Bjorn Again. The only question remaining as the afternoon wore on, exhilarating despite the pounding summer rain storm, was—would Nirvana themselves be appearing?

All week long, the British press had resounded with reports that the band had broken up, because of Kurt's ill-health, and the rumors were still circulating even as the roadies cleared off the stage in readiness for the headliners. Only when it seemed certain that Nirvana would be playing did that rumor finally die down, to be replaced by another—that this was to be their farewell show, "and don't expect too much excitement from Kurt, because my friend saw him backstage and he was seated in a wheelchair." Then the lights went down and sure enough—he was.

But he was out of it and playing like he'd never played before, like he'd maybe believed that he would never have the chance to play again. He was a man possessed, slamming the band through one of the most rigorous sets he'd played in years, a set which not only defied the health scare stories, but proved, too, that reports of Nirvana's demise had indeed been greatly exaggerated.

It was only those people who were closest to Kurt who really understood what was going through his mind, that he was playing his heart out because if he didn't, it would break. It later transpired that just 24 hours before he flew into England, Kurt and Courtney had been seriously contemplating suicide.

Only the hope that they might still win back Frances dissuaded them; that, and the knowledge that if they gave up now, then they needn't have fought so hard in the first place. They'd simply be proving that all their adversaries had been right in the first place.

8

O n September 8, Kurt and Courtney joined Chris and Dave at the 1992 MTV Music Video Awards. Nirvana, who were red hot favorites for both the Best New Artist and the Best Alternative Video awards with the Sam Bayer-directed "Teen Spirit", were to open the show, and were under the distinct impression that they could play what they wanted—that it didn't have to be one of the hits.

It was a condition the band themselves felt was of the utmost importance. All around them, even in the mere year or so since Nirvana had come to a position whereby they *could* dictate their own terms on occasion, the band had seen the entire Alternative ethos become so hopelessly, cripplingly corrupted that it was hard to believe it had ever embodied anything more than hollow words and gestures . . . and maybe, in fact, it hadn't.

It is, after all, one thing for a band to say they want to change the world when they can barely afford to change their own guitar strings; quite another for them to start rocking boats when they're out in mid-stream on the biggest boats of all. Here comes the new boss, same as the old Boss, and all that malarkey.

Soundchecking the day before the actual Awards ceremony, Nirvana ran through two new songs, one which

Kurt called "New Poopy", another which he titled "Rape Me". The impression was, this would be their choice for the show—and MTV freaked. "Rape Me" was out of the question, "New Poopy" was out of it too. The band could . . . should . . . *would* play "Teen Spirit".

No, the trio replied. If they couldn't play what they wanted, then they wouldn't play at all. And they meant it. There were no more than four hours to go before showtime.

Backstage, MTV's people were huddled together in one corner, Nirvana's entourage in another. Both understood the possible repercussions of this sudden, unexpected *impasse*.

From MTV's point of view, they would be beaming the world an awards ceremony which had already, after just a decade in operation, taken on the same kind of resonance as the Grammys—and they'd be doing so without one of the scheduled headline attractions. What would that do to their credibility? Especially when word got out about why Nirvana weren't appearing! At the same time, though, a new song would simply disappoint the millions of people who were tuning in simply to hear the songs they knew, and a new song called "Rape Me"—well, really! As show time grew inexorably nearer, the decision was reached—maybe they could compromise.

For Nirvana, the decision was no easier. Having railed in the past about the so-called alternative bands who so gratefully played the kiss-ass corporate rock game, what could be more kiss-ass, more corporate, than simply trotting out on stage and playing the big hit? There was no way they could do it.

But they also knew that the repercussions from their decision might not only affect their own strengths on the cable network, there were other people to consider too, beginning with Amy Finnerty, the programmer who first dropped "Teen Spirit" into the play lists and who had since adopted Nirvana almost as her own pet project. Could they allow themselves to become her pet liability also?

Then there were the other bands on Gold Mountain to consider, even the other bands on Geffen. Nobody doubted that if MTV really wanted to take a stand, they could threaten to ban an entire record company from their programming. Nirvana, too, bowed to the inevitable—maybe they could compromise also.

MTV made the first move—" 'Teen Spirit' or 'Lithium'." And Nirvana grabbed the olive branch gratefully . . . "Lithium". Only maybe they weren't as graceful as MTV liked to think they were being. The band was introduced, the audience was in raptures, and Kurt began to play . . . "rape me, rape me, my friend . . ." and then, without missing a beat, it was back to the scheduled programming, and if you missed those few seconds at the beginning of "Lithium", it was if Nirvana had done nothing wrong, and the MTV bigwigs who rushed to shut the cameras down could suddenly breathe again.

A Michael Jackson impersonator collected Nirvana's Best Alternative Video gong; but Kurt and Chris were finally prevailed upon to pick up the Best New Artist award themselves. Kurt looked shy, nervous, boyish, but he read off his thank yous, and he didn't throw up, shoot up, fall over, or do any of those things which a year of rumor and scandal and lies had primed his audience to expect. He didn't even sing forbidden songs. Instead, he looked deep into the camera, into every living room in America, and smiled. "You know, it's really hard to believe everything you read."

Two evenings later, Nirvana were back in Seattle, headlining a show at the Arena, and later, at Chris' behest, donating $25,000 of the proceeds to the Washington Music Industry Coalition, an anti-censorship group locked into what was to prove to be an 18-month battle against the state's so-called Erotic Music Bill, by which records could essentially be outlawed simply on the say-so of a single public complainant. (Ironically, the bill was finally defeated in the week following Kurt's suicide.)

With gestures like that to their credit, a second benefit in aid of the battle being waged against neighboring Oregon's anti-homosexual Proposition Nine, and the absurdly jocular *Ed Sullivan Show* take-off which Nirvana released as their latest video (accompanying "In Bloom"), adding their combined weight to Kurt's behavior at the MTV awards, it really did look as though Nirvana were turning their back on their so-tarnished image, and taking their abysmal luck with them.

Sub Pop were reportedly compiling a collection of Nirvana rarities, which would be released (in time for Christmas, 1992) in a bid to beat out the host of studio-quality bootlegs which had been surfacing over the past twelve months—a principle which Sony had already proven was eminently workable with their three CD Dylan collection, *The Bootleg Series*. After that, talk would turn to what was already the most eagerly antici-pated album of the decade so far, Nirvana's successor to *Nevermind*.

Frances was back with her parents, the hateful assaults from the tabloids had abated . . . and then the whole thing exploded again.

As lopsidedly symbiotic as rock'n'roll's relationship with celluloid may be, a dichotomous love affair which even Nirvana, shambling through Thurston Moore's *1991*, had failed to render on their own terms, the relationship between music and the world of publishing is even more fraught.

Rock books are not a new phenomena; the first "quickie" biographies of the top pop stars appeared almost as suddenly as the music itself, in the mid-1950s, when Elvis was still King, and the very name Presley was synonymous with goldmines. Since then, the market for rock biographies had grown as fast, maybe even faster than its host, voraciously scrambling for fact and scandal, learned tome and hardback tabloid side by side in the same artist's library, and the bigger the name, the harder they fought.

When Kurt and Courtney heard that a pair of British writers, Victoria Clarke and Britt Collins, were planning an allegedly no-holds-barred Nirvana biography, their immediate reaction was panic—after *Vanity Fair*, and the Family Court, and all the shit they'd been subjected to in the last twelve months, did all that count for nothing? Was it really only Round One?

It's unclear who took the offensive first, although the Nirvana camp was in no doubt that it was the writers, a belief which prompted John Silva, Nirvana's manager, to immediately—January 27th, 1992—contact everybody they could think of who could possibly have stories to tell . . . and ask them, please don't do it!

Silva's letter expressed Nirvana's own request that the letters' recipients "do not cooperate with these women in any way." The letters concluded, "Kurt, Chris and Dave would appreciate any assistance you can offer."

The battle intensified as the year wore on, and by late October, Kurt seems to have reached breaking point. Courtney had already contacted the writers, leaving a message on Clarke's answering machine in which she appears simply to have tried reasoning with them. The following night, it was Kurt's turn.

The full text of his messages (which Kurt originally publicly denied having left) was to keep the UK music press in rapture for weeks. Growing increasingly more abusive as his message—which was actually split over nine back-to-back calls, each of which took Clarke's machine to its two-minute message limit—he warned, "If anything comes out in this book which hurts my wife, I'll fucking kill you. . . ."

He and Courtney were still fighting to hang on to

their daughter; still lived in fear that any day, something could be published in the press that could launch the nightmare onto an even more nightmarish level. Regardless of the legal rights and wrongs of his threats, Kurt genuinely believed he was fighting for his family, and by extension of that, his life.

"At this point, I don't give a flying fuck if I have recorded that I'm threatening you. I suppose I could throw out a few hundred thousand dollars to have you snuffed out, but maybe I'll try it the legal way first."

Nine months later, with Nirvana having commissioned and (unlike Clarke and Collins) presided over the publication of their own "official" biography, Kurt remained unrepentant. Within the realms of what the band members and their families were willing to reveal, *Rolling Stone* writer Michael Azerrad's *Come As You Are* offered a remarkable recounting of the story-so-far (it concluded with the imminent release of *In Utero*), touching upon all the issues which had hitherto obsessed Nirvana's detractors, and offering serialization copywriters some of the juiciest cover lines they could hope for—as the UK publication, *Vox*, proved with its October 1993, cover story.

Emblazoned above a photo of Cobain, a stark headline bellowed "Kurt comes clean; 'I was just filling up the syringe as far as it could go without pulling the end off.'" With ironic serendipity, another, disconnected headline announced "Suicide *isn't* painless."

Who could resist a come-on like that? And regardless of whether or not Azerrad's book really was intended simply as a brilliantly orchestrated piece of damage limitation, at least one reviewer suggested, it did the trick. More than two years after John Silva first circulated his concerns about a proposed "unauthorized" Nirvana biography, Clarke and Collins' book remains unpublished.

October 1992, the month in which Kurt and Courtney's battle with a little slice of the Fourth Estate finally boiled out of control, continued to be tempestuous. The day before Halloween, Nirvana played their first show since the Arena gig six weeks earlier, headlining the massive Velez Sarsfield Stadium in Buenos Aires, Argentina.

It was a disaster. Infuriated by the sight and sound of 50,000 Argentineans hurling abuse and missiles at the all-female opening act, Portland's Calamity Jane (who broke up without playing another show, so devastating was their reception), Kurt essentially devoted his entire performance to feedback and noise, interspersed with half-hearted stabs at a few proper songs.

Not until he got together with William Burroughs to torture his guitar throughout twelve howling minutes of the beat author's "The Priest They Call Him" Christmas single, did Kurt recapture the sheer incandescent fury of the closing "Endless Nameless" . . . it was a mess, but that, Kurt insisted, was what the audience deserved. An incoherent mess.

Unfortunately, that same term could also be applied to the much-vaunted rarities collection, which appeared on schedule the week before Christmas 1992.

Although Nirvana themselves had been toying with the idea of such a collection since the first Butch Vig sessions two-and-a-half years before, the project only became viable in the wake of *Nevermind*, and when it became obvious that Nirvana's own schedule, private and musical, was going to keep them from the studio for much of 1992.

Originally, the project was Sub Pop's alone—*Cash Cow* (a title borrowed from a similarly much-anticipated Virgin Records various artists sampler of the early 1980s) would draw on the band's earlier, archive material—British radio sessions, hard-to-find singles, the original *Nevermind* demos and the like.

But logistically, Sub Pop simply did not have the

capacity to market what would undoubtedly prove such a monster-selling release, and when Geffen offered to combine the project with a similar compilation drawn from their own vaults, it made considerably sounder commercial sense—particularly as it would leave the door open for the two record companies to undertake a similar venture should the future ever demand it.

Unfortunately, the mixture did not sit well in the ears, lurching jarringly from brash metal to pure-bred pop, from jarring punk discordance to whatever one chose to call the defiantly uncategorizable sounds which had been ushered in by *Nevermind*.

Although the UK *Record Collector* welcomed the album with the kind of open arms one would expect from a magazine with such an uncomplicated title, *Incesticide* did not even reach gold status until February 1993, when Geffen released a video promoting one of the album cuts, the 1991 single "Sliver".

However, in other areas, it was to prove immensely influential.

The Raincoats were an occasionally all-girl group which flowered in the UK during the immediate post-Punk period at the end of the 1970s; formed in October 1977, the band joined label-mates the Pop Group and soul-mates the Slits in essentially redefining the course of the New Wave after the first purging napalm blast of Punk.

Kurt first heard the Raincoats during his early 1980s conversion to Punk, but his very own copy of their debut album had long since disappeared. The music continued to haunt him nevertheless; "Whenever I hear it, I'm reminded of a particular time in my life when I was . . . *extremely* unhappy, lonely and bored. If it wasn't for the luxury of putting on that scratchy copy of The Raincoats' first record, I would have had very few moments of peace."

Finally, according to his *Incesticide* liner notes (released to the press in the form of "an open letter from Kurt Cobain"), "I found myself in bloody exhaust grease London" in search of that "very-out-of-print LP."

A visit to the Rough Trade record label's own shop proved fruitless until Kurt spoke with the woman behind the counter. She told him she was a neighbor of Anna da Silva, and drew Kurt a map of how to get to the antique store where Anna now worked. Anna was at that store when Kurt arrived, "so I politely introduced myself with a fever-red face and explained the reason for my intrusion. She said, 'Well, I may have a few lying around, so if I find one, I'll send it to you.' I left feeling like a dork, like I had violated her space, like she probably thought my band was tacky."

Gina Birch, da Silva's fellow founder member, continues, "Anna dug out a copy, we all signed it and wrote little messages on it"; according to Kurt, receiving the gift "made me happier than playing in front of thousands of people each night."

This charming little interlude, a glimpse into the life of Kurt not as the "rock god" idol of millions, but as a red-faced fan seeking out an icon for his own collection, might have ended there, alongside the mentions of Kurt's other favorite bands, the Vaselines and Shonen Knife, the Melvins and the Stinky Puffs, in those same liner notes.

But something about his story seemed to touch people, the sense of sheer honesty which outshone even the dashes of black irony with which Kurt laced his words; an echo, even, of the impact "Teen Spirit" had had just fifteen short months before. In the UK, Rough Trade had long been planning a CD compilation of the Raincoats' finest moments; now, according to Birch, "I think [*Incesticide*] finally pushed them into doing something."

It also didn't hurt that Hole covered "The Void"— which Courtney would have learned from Anna's very gift—on a 1993 John Peel session, while according to

Birch's own sources, "Kurt's been caught playing it in rehearsal!"

It took another year, but shortly before Christmas, 1993, that precious first Raincoats album became the first installment of a full Raincoats' reissue program, handled by Rough Trade in Britain, Geffen in the US, and embracing all three of the albums released by this remarkable band prior to their 1984 split. Included in the packaging was another short essay from Kurt.

"The Raincoats were not very well-known in the States (according to Aspinall, they never got beyond the East Coast in two visits to the country)—I don't know about the UK and Europe. In fact, I really don't know anything about the Raincoats. . . ."

It was the pleasure of being able to reawaken interest in his own musical favorites, of being able to educate even a handful of people into the sounds which he considered worth hearing, which Kurt once described as "making a lot of the other shit worthwhile"—he could also claim much of the credit for reawakening interest in the Vaselines, the rag-tag Scots duo who celebrated the release of their debut album by breaking up.

Since then, they had reformed just once—to open for Nirvana in Edinburgh, at Kurt's own nervous request; Eugene Kelly, meanwhile, had formed a new band, Captain America, which metamorphosed into Eugenius in late 1992. Again, the band deserved to break out on its own substantial merits, but Kurt's widely proclaimed interest certainly didn't go amiss. The press release for Eugenius' 1993 *Mary, Queen of Scots* album concludes, "For more info and classic 'Don't Believe The Hype Stories,' call. . . ."

If *Incesticide* brought 1992 to a somewhat uninspiring close, the new year dawned with inspired madness—two shows in Brazil, in Sao Paulo and Rio, in mid-late January. Nirvana were in a playful mood. "Seasons in the Sun", Jacques Brel's mysteriously doom-laden farewell to life, proved an unexpected addition to a bristling set; so did a rendition of Duran Duran's "Rio", worked up especially for the occasion, with Dave hamming it up delightedly at the microphone, while Kurt played drums and Chris, guitar.

Later in the show, the Red Hot Chili Peppers' Flea, a close friend of Kurt and Courtney's even before his own infant daughter, Clara, took little Frances Bean under her five year-old wing, turned up on stage to play a trumpet solo in the midst of "Teen Spirit".

Nirvana returned to the States immediately after the Brazilian gigs were over; they had a month with their families, and then it was into the studio to begin work, at last, on *Nevermind*'s successor.

The majority of the record was already written, salvaged from the sludge-filled tub which had greeted Kurt and Courtney when they returned from Spain, more was left over from the *Nevermind* sessions, and just needing a little up-dating to make them fit the new album. Several of the songs were already live favorites, and "Rape Me" (one of the *Nevermind*-era tracks) had already been given a serious shot of publicity thanks to the MTV Video *contretemps*.

What most intrigued about this latest project, then, was the band's choice of producer, Steve Albini—not least of all because according to Albini himself, the first *he* knew about the engagement was when he read about it in the UK music press a full six months before Nirvana even contacted him! At one point, the speculation grew so intense that he actually contacted the magazines in question, fervently denying the rumor. It was within a few days of that, that Gold Mountain contacted him.

"No one who knows me is surprised that I was not the biggest fan of *Nevermind*," Albini admits, describing that album as having become "so unavoidable that it became a nuisance." At the same time, though, "people I knew who knew them kept telling me what great people they were, and that's how it turned out. They were very well prepared coming into the studio, as prepared as any band I've worked with, and as easy to deal with as any band I've worked with."

Unlike Butch Vig at the time he masterminded *Nevermind*, Albini already had a considerable track record, with major and indie labels alike. The last PJ Harvey album, *Rid of Me*, was one of his, as was Silkworm's then-forthcoming *In The West*. He'd worked with the Pixies, and with England's Wedding Present—a band which chalked up the enviable record of releasing twelve consecutive British singles in the space of one year, only to get dropped by their record label at the end of that period; and with Pigface, a band whose sound was as brutal as their name.

But before all that, he'd been the guiding light behind Big Black, one of the seminal bands of early '80s' America, and his reputation behind the mixing desk today remains as uncompromising as that he enjoyed before an audience ten years before. Most people who heard of his union with Nirvana thought the whole concept was total madness.

"In print and on TV, Nirvana had given the world the finger," *Alternative Press* explained. "What were the odds against them doing the same on CD? And what hope that Albini, a man whose entire *raison d'etre* screams 'base primitivism' . . . , would even try to stop them? On the face of it, none." In terms of commercial potential, the magazine continued, "it was a marriage made in audio hell."

The notion that Nirvana's next album, originally titled *Verse Chorus Verse*, but eventually settling down as *In Utero*, would be a basic "fuck you" to the music industry had been in circulation for close to twelve months now. Kurt's own behavior, through that year of almost inhuman pressures and demands, had increasingly pointed towards an eruption of some kind, and memories of the band's October show in Buenos Aires, when Kurt came offstage marveling at the sheer intensity of the noises he had wrung from his guitar, were not difficult to subvert.

Clearly, the same idea occurred to Albini as he figured out his own demands for what could conceivably turn into a very rigorous series of sessions. His requirements were simple, but somewhat unconventional. For starters, he was not to be referred to as the album's producer—standard Albini practice, but virtually unheard of in typical major label circles. Instead, Albini required the simple credit "recorded by . . .".

Financially, too, he was unusual. On top of studio costs, Albini charged $100,000 for what would prove two weeks work. His high rates were balanced by the fact that it would be a one-time-only fee. He expected no royalties. It was a deal he liked to cut with every band he worked with—on the one hand, it ensured that he got paid for his work all at once, and didn't have to wait around for statements and checks; on the other hand, it adhered to his own belief that "anyone who takes a royalty off a band's record, other than someone who actually writes music or plays on the record, is a thief."

He also insisted that a contract be drawn up, prohibiting anybody—and that included the band themselves—from interfering with the finished recording, without his express permission. It was done, he said later, to protect Nirvana—knowing that Geffen were unhappy about his selection as producer, he envisioned the band being pushed to bring someone else in to remix the record. This contract would later become the source of considerable aggravation for Albini and Nirvana.

Still milking a favorite old joke of Kurt's, the band booked into Pachyderm Studios, outside Minneapolis, under the hotel room pseudonym of The Simon Ritchie Group. Geffen were prohibited from attending the sessions—aside from a few days when Courtney dropped by, the group's only company for the entire two week stint comprised Albini and his assistant, Bob Weston.

Nirvana slipped effortlessly into Albini's regimen. "I like to make people as comfortable as possible," the producer says, "and that doesn't mean indulging their every whim, it means making life as normal as possible."

Instead of filling the studio with industry top-dogs, "I try to make it like day-to-day life—get up in the morning and have breakfast, go to the studio, work, play, set Dave Grohl on fire, then back to the house to eat dinner and watch wildlife videos." During the course of the sessions, Dave saw his hat, hair and pants go up in smoke, in between finding out more than he could ever possibly have wanted to know about "the sex life of sea anenomes."

So far, so good. But no sooner was the record completed than reports began to appear, primarily in the UK press, in which the album was described not only as a turkey, but as a totally unacceptable turkey. A year earlier, in an interview with *Rip*, Kurt had joked of Nirvana's sudden critical fame, "I'm looking forward to some backlash, some criticism, because there's so much anticipation that I'm afraid." He was about to get all the criticism he could stomach.

The UK magazine *Select* did a very thorough job in covering the rumors which were suddenly flying back and forth, beginning with the apocryphal story of Nirvana playing their new album to their label and being told, "Great demos—but when can we expect to hear the finished album?"

"I was actually having journalists call up, saying, 'We understand you've ruined the new Nirvana album,' " Albini repeats incredulously, but at the end of the day Kurt insisted, "I can honestly say that only one person in the entire Geffen organization, at least among the people we worked with, had anything to say *against* the album."

That was Gary Gersh, the group's long-time A&R man (who later quit the company to assume control at Capitol Records). "He didn't like it for various sonic reasons. But he heard the album before it was mastered, and it's at that stage that a lot of those problems can be sorted out. Which is basically what Albini said to begin with."

There do, however, seem to have been some other complaints—Kurt told Michael Azerrad that a number of Geffen and Gold Mountain staff disliked the record intensely ("the grown-ups don't like it," he smirked mischievously), and it was easy to glean fresh inferences from the band's decision to remix two of the tracks, "No Apologies" and Kurt's ode to Courtney, "Heart-shaped Box".

According to Chris, however, that latter was his do-ing, and nobody else's—in its original form, the song had a lengthy effects-laden solo carving through it, a solo which Novoslic admits made his flesh crawl simply to think about. "The band would say something, how great the album was, and it was like—'yeah, shame about that solo, though.' "

Finally, Kurt and Dave agreed to excise the offending solo, and this, as *Alternative Press* commented, "is where things go awry. It's now common knowledge that the band and Albini had a contractual agreement which stipulated that no work could be done on the album once Albini declared it finished. It's less widely known, apparently, that Albini happily waived that stipulation the moment Cobain asked him about it."

Scott Litt, one of Geffen's original choices for *Never-mind*, and now one of Chris's favorite producers, ever since he heard R.E.M's *Automatic for the People*, eventually came in to handle the remixing (later, Litt would also produce Hole's *Live Through This* album), but only after Albini had been offered the job himself. He turned it down because "I thought I'd already given it my best shot."

"Having me work on the record any more wouldn't change anything, so they asked if it would be okay for them to go in and work on it with Scott Litt, and I didn't see any reason not to let them." Like Nirvana, he remains mystified how so straightforward an arrangement could have been blown up, in the pages of the press, into a major dispute between band and producer.

Geffen, too, seemed stunned by the speculation. "We will release whatever record the band deliver," Geffen president Ed Rosenblatt announced. "It's that boring and straightforward." To add credence to the message, Rosenblatt's comments were released to the media on official Geffen stationery beneath the headline, "Nirvana's Kurt Cobain debunks rumors of Geffen interference with new album."

Throughout the sessions for *In Utero*, Chris was busy writing an article for *Spin* magazine on the conflict which was (and still is) destroying his Croatian homeland. Now, with the album over, he persuaded Kurt and Dave to join him at a benefit show for the Tresnjevka Womens' Center in Zagreb, to be staged at San Francisco's Cow Palace on April 9th. They agreed, and Nirvana's presence on the bill, alongside L7, the Breeders and the Disposable Heroes of Hip-hop-risy, helped raise some $50,000 for rape victims of alleged Serbian "ethnic cleansing" atrocities.

Even as its release date approached, the publicity surrounding the launch of Nirvana's third album continued to fixate upon the supposed rift with Albini—when the first prerelease copies of *In Utero* reached the press, then, many people were surprised by the sheer variety, and texture, of the record. It wasn't simple boasting which prompted Kurt to describe the album as at least the equal of—and in some places, superior to—*Nevermind*.

He was adamant from the beginning that the album would be presented to the public "as an album. I'm so sick of records which, when you listen to them, could have been thrown together at the last minute. Even though everything's on one side on CDs now, records should still have a distinct first side, second side. When I listen to an album, I listen to it as a solid body of work, 40 minutes in a life rather than ten four-minute excerpts. There's always songs I like more than others, but the point is, they all have their place on the album, and if they don't, then the album doesn't work. Not as an album."

Chris later admitted that the band spent almost as long getting the songs in the right order as they did recording the thing. " 'Rape Me' was the original album opener, but we moved it because it has a similar intro to 'Teen Spirit', and if people *have* to say we've just repeated *Nevermind*, we'd rather they don't get that chance right away."

It was to maintain this sense of continuity that two songs originally scheduled for inclusion on the album, the erstwhile title cut "Verse, Chorus, Verse", and the seemingly self-explanatory "I Hate Myself and Want to Die", were ultimately omitted from the record, while "Tourrette's", 90 seconds of bellowing and profanity which Kurt admitted "isn't even that good a song" (and which was originally titled "Chuck Chuck") was left in place. "It fit the mood," he said, a mood which was as complex, and as changeable, as Cobain himself.

If there was a theme to the album, it was that of alienation within a world totally beyond Kurt's control or creation, laced with a sly cynicism against which Albini's bass-heavy production slammed itself with increasing rage.

The opening lines of the first track, "Serve the Servants", summed up a lot of Cobain's own feelings— "teenage angst" had indeed "paid off well", but the

key lyric came in the chorus when he opined that
the "legendary divorce"—the break-up of his parents to
which so many of his current emotional problems were
now being traced—had become "such a bore."

No single event in his life had brought him to this
current confused, angry, hurt state of mind; it was a
combination of many, and if the divorce—and the ensuing bouncing around between sundry different relatives—was the moment at which his family noticed that
Kurt was a considerably deeper, and considerably more
disturbed, child than they had hitherto reckoned, elsewhere *In Utero* boasted more than one suggestion
("Dumb", with its weary confession that "I'm not like
them, but I can pretend") that that had simply been its
public unveiling. Tracing his behavior through since
childhood, there was very little room for pretense.

Yet there is no doubting that the divorce was a catalyst.

"Since the age of seven [his parents broke up when he
was eight, but their difficulties surely began sooner], I've
become hateful to all humans in general," he wrote in
his farewell to the world—and why? "Because I love and
feel for people too much."

In the midst of his pain, perhaps even a cause of his
pain, it hurt him even more that people simply couldn't
get on with one another. On *Nevermind*, the anthemic
(and in its own way, equally revelatory) "Territorial
Pissings" opens with Chris singing a snatch from the
Youngbloods' "Get Together"—come on everybody, you
gotta love one another . . . It was a joke, but was it a
coincidental one?

Kurt was beginning to unravel, personally if not musically. Desperation haunts *In Utero*—one seasoned observer was heard to complain, upon hearing *In Utero* for
the first time, "Oh God, he's written a Pain of Fame
album already", and although it is worth noting that the
songs which most obviously fit that condemnation were

those which had been around since *before* fame came knocking ("Rape Me", and the punningly titled "Penny Royal Tea"), that construction, too, had its place. ("Penny Royal", incidentally, is also a homeopathic abortion treatment.)

The handful of interviews which Nirvana gave in America and Europe around the time of *In Utero*'s release each presented Kurt in a state of withdrawal from (if not total denial of) his status, to the point where the band as a whole seemed to have wholly divorced itself from its fame.

Discussing the events of the past eighteen months, all three members of the band consistently referred to *Nevermind*'s breakthrough, or that of "Teen Spirit" as if it were a separate entity, and that neither had anything to do with Nirvana. They had completely divorced themselves from their own fame.

Chris put it very clearly when he talked to *Alternative Press* in July. "We came along as a time of great change, politically and socially. Suddenly all the people who'd been waving yellow ribbons during the Gulf War were wondering what it was for, how things had changed because of it. And when they found they couldn't answer those questions, they got angry."

"Teen Spirit" tapped into that anger, or maybe reflected it. *Nevermind* picked up the slack. The fact that Nirvana themselves got sucked into the maelstrom along with their records was simply an unavoidable, and unfortunate, side-effect.

The very morality of the situation, too, haunted Kurt. He once admitted that it was his greatest dream for Nirvana to tour with Sonic Youth—a dream which was to come true on several occasions, of course. Now, his nightmare was that one day the roles would be reversed, and Sonic Youth would have to support Nirvana. Geffen had already raised the question, and so far Kurt had managed to hold off. But how much longer could he keep stonewalling like that?

"It's not that I'm scared they'll blow us off stage, because I know they probably will. It's the fact that without Sonic Youth's examples, there'd probably be no Nirvana." It didn't matter that a support slot on a Nirvana tour would probably do Sonic Youth's own commercial standing the power of good. Some things were simply wrong.

One incident, however, vividly illustrates Kurt's own rejection, or perhaps, total non-acceptance, of his own position.

In July 1993, Seattle journalist Jo-Ann Greene was press-ganged into driving another writer into downtown Seattle to interview Nirvana. The interview had been scheduled and rescheduled several times, and both writers fully expected this latest date to go the same way as its predecessors. Dropping her companion at the designated hotel, Greene parked her car, then rejoined him at the hotel, to see if the interview was actually going ahead.

It was; Nirvana were already in the hotel lobby, so Greene walked over to let her passenger know she was leaving.

"Kurt, standing between Chris Novoselic and Dave Grohl, spotted me [immediately]. I smiled, and he immediately dropped his gaze.

"As the distance between us shortened [it was never more than ten yards or so], Kurt's unease became apparent. His eyes darted back and forth, he hunched [deeper] into his own shoulders. By the time I was half way there, Kurt was beginning to sidle backwards. I kept walking—our gaze met again. This time, his eyes showed naked terror; he looked like a cornered animal. I dropped my eyes and looked instead at his bandmates, who appeared either unaware or unconcerned. Grohl looked up and smiled.

"In those couple of seconds, Kurt slid behind the much larger Novoselic. Smiling back at Grohl, I reached the group and said, 'I'm off. Bye guys.' Novoselic and Grohl both smiled again, I turned and walked away. Several steps later I could hear Kurt's audible sigh of relief behind me."

Talking to the writer afterwards, Greene continues, he simply laughed and said, "Yeah I saw it, you almost scared him to death!"

Chris and Dave, however, reacted—or rather, didn't react—in a way which suggested this was Cobain's "normal" behavior, but it was to be another ten months before Greene says she truly appreciated just how abnormal Kurt's normalcy was. His suicide note made it perfectly apparent that he was incapable of handling the pressure of stardom—but his behavior had made that obvious for a long time. Following that brief encounter, there was "absolutely no doubt" in Greene's mind either. For Kurt, she says, "the unbearable continued as 'normal', until the unbearable could not be borne anymore."

And as the recorded voice of Courtney Love floated over the Seattle Center at Kurt's April 10th memorial and, in a moment of unguarded bitterness she led the crowd in a chant of "Asshole", Greene later wrote, "Asshole? No. What I saw was a terribly frightened, obviously disturbed man, whose hunted eyes will haunt me now forever."

9

The barracking was muted at first, an unsettling murmur at the back of the hall. A lone voice cried "play some rock'n'roll," and Cobain looked up from his acoustic guitar, his unnaturally blue, piercing eyes focusing in the darkness. Dylan got it in Newport, Bowie in Philadelphia. But Nirvana in New York? JUDAS!

A week before in Seattle, Cobain spoke excitedly of introducing a short acoustic set into Nirvana's live show. "A lot of people miss the point, that not all our songs are shrieking punk rock monsters," he smiled. " 'Unplugged' is something of a buzz word right now, but if you do it properly. . . . "

At the New Music Seminar, Nirvana did do it properly. But a cello-powered "Polly", aching into a second song, breaking to a third—after a "Territorial Pissings" which set 3,000 onlookers ablaze, a four-song set-closer which didn't even break sweat was just too hard for most folk to take. The isolated catcalls ganged together and howled. A few more people booed. "PLAY SOME ROCK'N'ROLL!"

Afterwards, Kurt would admit that he could hear people talking throughout the acoustic performance, that at times they'd sounded louder than the band. "Very rude. I mean, even if I don't like a band that much, I'd still have enough respect not to do that. But I guess that's New York for you." But fuck them. Nirvana had never given way to that sort of pressure in the past—they weren't about to start now. The acoustic set would remain in the show.

"I don't want to react in such an extreme way as maybe U2 have, by turning their show into a kitsch vaudeville act and being so sarcastic about the whole idea of being a rock'n'roll star that it becomes a joke." Because it *wasn't* a joke for Kurt—it was his livelihood and, by some strange, compulsory extension of that, his very life.

Over and over as she read Kurt's suicide note into the microphone, a mere nine months later, Courtney could not help but interject her own replies to the questions which Kurt left hanging—if he hated what he did so much, why didn't he just stop?

Because he couldn't, because he wouldn't be allowed to. There is something incredibly romantic about the idea of simply casting the world aside and becoming a recluse—from Howard Hughes to Brian Wilson, and on to Pink Floyd's Syd Barrett, regardless of their own personal motives or state of mind, all three essentially took a powder at the peak of their powers, pulled themselves away from the rock'n'roll (or in Hughes' case, Hollywood) circus and sank gracefully into legend.

But how peaceful was their retirement? Hughes became the subject of gossip, and tales of his eccentricities still circulate today. Wilson became the object of wild speculation, and Barrett, that of such fanatical mythology that even his former band mates were still writing songs about him *seven years* after he left the band, and the occasions when he did venture out of his home became major events in the eyes of the press—and by extension, it seems, in Barrett's own mind as well.

A fanzine devoted to him even featured a regular column titled "Syd Sightings", as though he was a UFO or something, then filled it with tales which ranged from the distinctly plausible to the utterly unimaginable. If Kurt ever did consider the possibility of simply stepping back and allowing the madness to recede, the Syd Barrett story would certainly have given him pause for contrary thought.

So he carried on, bitterly, resentfully, sadly, but with sufficient self-control (and stubborn contrariness) that he could hide his deepest, darkest feelings from the people who were in the best position to help him.

Courtney's sob-choked reaction to his last words suggests that even she was not aware quite how low her husband was sinking as Nirvana toured the United States and Europe in the wake of *In Utero*'s October 1993 release. That is hardly surprising—he was away from home much of the time, and when the couple were together, on the road in hotels or backstage at gigs, and briefly in Atlanta during the recording of Hole's next album, so much else would be going on around them that even if she was prepared to listen to his problems, Kurt would not have been comfortable talking about them.

The Clarke-Collins book controversy had receded into the background, somewhat, but they were not the only journalists on Kurt Cobain's trail. Even off-duty, Kurt needed to remain on-guard.

There were some happy moments. Driving back to the band's hotel after one American show, Kurt suddenly announced that he was hungry and wanted to stop at a Taco Bell he could see a short way off.

One of the people who were helping shepherd the band around, looked horrified. "You can't go in there! It's 11:30 at night, the gig's just turned out, the place will be packed!"

But Kurt was adamant. It had been a good show, he was in a good mood, and he was hungry. "Stop the car. Let's go."

With every nerve screaming in trepidation, Kurt's companion followed Kurt into the crowded restaurant—"and I'd never seen him so happy. He just sat there signing autographs, talking with fans, having a wonderful time."

In the days following Kurt's death, a lot of stories like that began emerging, inching out from beneath the pall of "sad, misunderstood genius" epitaphs which the media were now heaping upon Kurt's poor, martyred head—the times he would pause for a photograph, smile and sign autographs, accept even the most unexpected interruption with a grace and civility a million miles removed from the self-absorbed monster which he was so often painted in the media.

"Maybe he was a junkie, maybe he was messed up, maybe he did do all the things the papers said he did," said one. "But he was a human being as well, and he showed that a lot more often than he was given credit for."

Nirvana spent much of fall, 1993, on tour in the US, an outing—like the European gigs which would follow in the new year—which was considerably longer than Kurt would ever have wished. Still, he never put his foot down; reports from across the country spoke of how well Nirvana were playing, how intense the performances were, and most of all, how hyped up on it all Kurt appeared to be.

The band had once again added a second guitarist: Big John of English Oi! legends The Exploited sat in with them in New York; now they were joined by Pat Smear, once the motivating guitar roar behind the legendary Germs. Now Kurt was so much freer to concentrate on his vocals, and he obviously relished the opportunity.

Backstage, he was less voluble—tour insiders speak of long periods of withdrawn silence which may or may not have been giving way to depression; even if one is fully qualified to determine the state of another person's mind, it is often difficult to pinpoint the precise malady, particularly when the sufferer will not speak.

But while the cloak of silence which surrounds Kurt's state of mind during these last months remains impenetrable, it is clear that both Geffen and Gold Mountain were growing increasingly concerned with Kurt, as a business proposition—he was, after all, earning them one hell of a lot of money, but also as a human being.

Confronted in the days immediately following Kurt's death with the accusation that the people who should have been doing the most to ensure Kurt remained on an even-footing were widely perceived as having done too little, a visibly shaken Geffen insider insisted that a great deal had been done, and even more had been offered. "But how can you help someone who doesn't want to be helped, who rejects every overture which is made to him?"

Locked into his own cycle of incredible ups and crippling downs (a recognized symptom of the manic depression which many people have since speculated Kurt was suffering from), Kurt either had no *need* for that assistance, because he was feeling good and the world was his oyster, or no *faith* in it, convinced that the only instincts he could trust were his own, and that everybody else simply wanted to get a piece of him for their own sake.

In his position, he knew, he was both a person and a commodity—among the most important requirements of stardom is an ability to instinctively separate oneself sufficiently from those attributes to know which one the people around you are addressing. Kurt did not have that ability. When he was "up", everyone was his friend, and he viewed those who surrounded him with implicit trust. Interviewers who caught him during these periods came away feeling they had made a friend for life.

But when he was "down", everyone was out to get him.

He rejected the suggestion that he be given a bodyguard to protect him from the intrusions of fans, reporters and the like, because that was not what Punk Rock was all about. According to one insider, he continued to believe that Nirvana were separate from the mainstream music industry, even as they adhered to mainstream industry practices, even as they recorded *ipso facto* mainstream music—what other description, after all, can be applied to a band whose last two albums have been worldwide number ones?

"Axl Rose has a bodyguard," Kurt once sneered when the subject was broached. "I'm not Axl Rose."

In an interview published just weeks before Kurt's death, Courtney attempted to explain his attitude to *Spin* magazine. Eddie Van Halen, guitarist with the eponymous Metal band, turned up backstage at a Nirvana show, "and practically begged to join them onstage for the encore, completely oblivious to the fact that bands like Nirvana exist partly to destroy dinosaurs like himself."

Seventeen years previous, the Sex Pistols, The Adverts, and their fellow first-wave Punk bands had set out with similar purpose in mind. Could Nirvana succeed where they had failed? Only time would tell. Unfortunately, time was something Kurt had very little left of.

In October, Nirvana fulfilled Kurt's earlier promise of doing something along the lines of *MTV Unplugged* when they appeared on . . . *MTV Unplugged*.

Broadcast around the same time as the Portland-based independent label, Tim/Kerr Records, finally released Kurt's collaboration with William Burroughs, "The Priest They Called Him", *MTV Unplugged* was a relaxed, joyous occasion.

Joined as usual by second guitarist Smear, and cellist Lori Goldstein (from Seattle's Black Cat Orchestra), Nirvana performed a lengthy set which drew not only upon their own repertoire, but also that of sundry friends.

Included were a Vaselines' song, two Meat Puppets' classics (with guest appearances from that band's Cris and Curt Kirkwood, introduced by Kurt as "the brothers Meat Puppet"), even a David Bowie number, "The Man Who Sold The World"—prefaced by Kurt with the warning, "I guarantee you I will screw this song up", (he didn't!) and graced with a curiously apposite ad lib, mid-verse: "I gazed a gazeless stare with multi-millionaires, I must have died alone, a long, long time ago."

Nirvana were back before the MTV cameras at the end of the year, when they were booked to co-headline the station's annual New Year Eve's concert with Pearl Jam.

It was a wry pairing. Pearl Jam, forged from the mid-'80s Seattle band Green River and Mother Love Bone, had emerged into the limelight just months after Nirvana's breakthrough, and in terms of button-counting record sales, had eclipsed even *Nevermind*'s astonishing statistics.

It was not jealousy, however, which prompted Kurt to lambast Pearl Jam at every opportunity. Like the possibility of Sonic Youth having to open for Nirvana on tour, it was a moral dilemma, and Kurt knew exactly where he fell on that score.

"I feel a duty to warn the kids about false music that's claiming to be underground or alternative," he told *Rolling Stone*, and having already described Pearl Jam as "the ones responsible for this corporate, alternative and cock-rock fusion", he now added, "They're just jumping on the alternative bandwagon."

The truth to the matter, of course, cuts both ways—just as 1977, and the first flowering of British Punk, saw a vast number of bands emerge on the scene whose own Punk credentials were questionable to say the very least,

but who were nevertheless welcomed into the burgeoning new community, so the outpouring of assuredly
"alternative" bands in the early 1990s had seen a similar
blurring of labels and boundaries. Nirvana themselves
had been scooped up by musical communities far removed from their own chosen place—their videos
showed up on *Headbangers Ball*, their pictures appeared
in *Metal Hammer* and *Kerrang!*, they were even offered a
slot on a Guns n'Roses/Metallica tour (which they declined). In fairness to Pearl Jam, the precise same things
had happened to them.

The feud which rankled between Nirvana and Pearl
Jam rose and fell according to the two bands' own public
visibility; in late 1993, both had just released their much-
anticipated follow-ups to the multi-platinum breakthrough albums, both had seen their records enter the
Billboard charts at #1. The MTV concert was to be their
chance to finally, publicly, bury the hatchet—only Pearl
Jam left it at home.

As showtime appeared, the Pearl Jam entourage was
appearing more and more restless—Eddie Vedder, the
band's vocalist, had still to appear; did not, in fact, turn
up at all. Nirvana played alone. Hopes that they and
Pearl Jam might come together on stage for a frenzied
New Year encore disappeared, and instead, it became
Vedder's turn to be the subject of the wildest media
speculation as to his whereabouts. Kurt certainly cracked
a smile over that one—he could not have known that just
four months later, he would be the object of an even
more frenzied manhunt . . . and he wouldn't turn up
with the flu at the end of it.

Nirvana's British and European dates were remarkable
for the sheer sense of history with which the band
bolstered the show. In London, they were supported by
the Raincoats, reforming around original members Anna
da Silva and Gina Birch, as a direct consequence of

Kurt's own interest; on the continent, another reformed Punk legend, the Buzzcocks, joined the bill.

Most every evening, Kurt would be spotted either alongside the stage, or incognito in the audience, simply lapping up Pete Shelley's bitter-sweet high octane love songs . . . and maybe slipping back into the teenaged misfit who once lay in his room, identifying with every word Shelley sang.

The Melvins played a number of these shows as well, joining Nirvana on tour just months after Kurt had joined them in the studio to produce their seventh album, and major label debut, *Houdini*.

In the years since the Melvins split the Northwest for San Francisco, much had happened, including an unprecedented surge of interest in the group after Kurt went on *Saturday Night Live* wearing one of their T-shirts. "You couldn't buy better advertising," Buzz Osbourne later laughed, but more was to come.

When asked about his formative musical influences, Kurt always thanked the Melvins. When pressed to predict the future of rock'n'roll, it was the Melvins again. Now he was about to make his debut as a producer, and though the pressures of *In Utero*'s painfully ballyhooed birth eventually hauled him out of the studio with the job only partially complete, Dale Crover says, Kurt definitely had some interesting ideas, things he'd learned about different mikes, treatments, tunings. But generally he'd just leave us to it. He was an ideas man—[which is] the best sort of producer, at least for a band like us."

The end of the tour was looming. On February 22nd, the band played a blinding show in Rome, one of the best they had played all tour. The next stop, Milan, however, was disastrous. Over the course of two shows, Kurt neither looked, nor played, like himself—"he looked dead on stage", one observer remarked.

He was little better when the tour reached Germany for the final shows; Kurt came off-stage at the conclusion of the final night, in Munich on March 1st, and the look in his eyes said more than words ever could. He couldn't, wouldn't, play another concert if his life depended upon it.

From Munich, Kurt flew to Rome, where he was meeting up with Courtney. The couple was booked into the Excelsior Hotel, and the visit was intended as nothing more than a little well-deserved rest and recreation.

Within days, the flashbulbs would be popping brighter than they ever had in the past.

Epilogue

Amazingly, no one seems to have heard, or at least noticed, the shot. Two days later, on Thursday, April 7th, the Seattle Police Department reportedly received another summons to the Cobain residence, when a phone call alleging a disturbance was apparently received. Five minutes later, a source insists, a second call retracted it, insisting that the report was merely a hoax.

The police would have responded either way, but the house was silent, empty, and the workmen who had been in the grounds throughout the week wouldn't have known anything about disturbances or hoax calls. So far as they were concerned, Mr. and Mrs. Cobain hadn't been near the house all week. The private detectives who were still engaged in searching for Kurt would have backed up their story, and so would the neighbors. Cobain's body lay where he fell for three days.

Back in L.A., Courtney was at her wits' end. A full week had now passed since she last spoke with her husband. She was, her lawyer, Barry Tarlow, later said, already "disturbed, concerned, troubled"; now she was allegedly having some kind of allergic reaction to the medication prescribed for her, to try and sooth her nerves. Hives and swellings were breaking out on her body. Desperately, she called 911.

Courtney was rushed to Century City hospital, not, however, as an allergy sufferer, but as a suspected drug overdose. Following treatment, she was booked on suspicion of narcotics possession; possession of drug paraphernalia (including a hypodermic needle); and possession of stolen property—a prescription book, Tarlow said, which her doctor had left behind in her room.

He also dismissed the possession charge. Tarlow said the fine powder, which the authorities found in a good-luck charm, was ashes.

Courtney was released on $10,000 bail three hours after she was charged. Arraignment was set for May 5. She resumed her vigil.

But her wait was almost over.

Gary Smith, a 50-year-old electrician employed by Veca Electrical Contractors in Bellevue, arrived at the Cobain house around 8:30 A.M. on Friday, April 9th, to begin installing a security system.

"I walked around to the door on the back side of the garage [and] looked to see if I had a way to route the wire." That's when he saw the body, "through a glass opening in the door." Except at first, he didn't know it was a body. At first, he thought it was a dressmaker's mannequin lying alongside an upturned flowerpot.

Then he saw the blood, congealed in the right ear. And then he saw the shotgun, pointing at the chin.

Smith bolted for his truck and put a call through to the dispatcher. "Call 911 . . . there's a body!" He admitted that he didn't recognize it, that he'd never seen Kurt Cobain. "If he passed me on the street, I would not know who he was."

While Smith waited for the police to arrive, his boss was on the phone to local rock radio station KXRX-FM.

"He had his details straight," says DJ Beau Roberts, who took the call. "But when I asked him his name, he was very defensive and hung up. We thought it was just another hoax." It would not, after all, have been the first time—rumor mills thrive on death and disaster, and it really doesn't need much to start the ball rolling.

It took a second, more detailed, call to convince KXRX to take their inquiries further; then, when the police department confirmed that a body had indeed been discovered, the station broadcast what information they had, breaking the news to a stunned Seattle.

It was precious little, but more than enough. Throughout the day, listeners remained glued to radio sets for updates, info, or even vague rumor. MTV went into day-long overdrive, prompting *Time* magazine to compare their coverage with that which followed the assassination of JFK, 31 years before—"with Kurt Loder in the role of Walter Cronkite."

Still, as late as its mid-afternoon edition, the local *Seattle Times* newspaper still couldn't provide anything more concrete than the fact that a body had indeed been discovered; and the police were keeping quiet as well. There was a suicide note, but police "wouldn't say who signed [it], who it was addressed to, or its contents. They [also] declined to discuss the identity of the dead man."

For Cobain's audience, however, even the rumor was enough. By 11:30 A.M., the first knot of fans were braving the drizzle and making their way to Madrona. By mid-afternoon, though there were still no more than half a dozen milling around, the most disinterested passerby would have noticed that something very tragic, very sad, had just shattered the peace of the leafy, well-heeled neighborhood.

Things were somewhat more frantic elsewhere. At one point, crisis hotlines in Seattle were taking up to quarter of an hour to answer their phones, and as late as midnight, there was still a lengthy delay. One volunteer worker admitted she had never experienced a day like it—and hoped she never would again.

Three days later, on Monday, April 11th, the first copycat suicide was reported in Seattle. It would not be the last. "Cobain was a talented artist, but his last message implied suicide was okay," King County Executive Gary Lock complained to the media. "It's crucial [now] that we answer that message. There is help available." MTV backed his message by including an item on suicide prevention in the following weekend's *Week In Rock* news show.

Both KXRX and KISW announced that they would be broadcasting Nirvana's music throughout the weekend, pre-empting their scheduled programming and playlists. "People are just in shock," KXRX news director Mike West said. "For the so-called 'Generation X', he's the John Lennon of their time. They lived for every word."

KISW DJ Mike Jones agreed. The station's switchboard had been ringing red-hot all day, hundreds of fans calling, "not wanting to hear what we have to tell them. They expect us to tell them it's a rumor."

But of course, it wasn't. By the end of the day, KXRX, KISW and KNDD had announced they would be staging a memorial vigil at the Seattle Center Flag Pavilion for Sunday evening. Saturday night, there would be a candlelight vigil in Cobain's Aberdeen hometown, while local label Sub Pop's long-scheduled sixth birthday party, set to be staged at the Crocodile Cafe that same evening, was now being referred to as a wake. The news cameras were outside before the invited guests even started arriving.

It was a subdued, and for the assembled pressmen, a disappointing affair. Three bands played, all Sub Pop discoveries—Sunny Day Real Estate, Pond and Velocity Girl—but even their own fans seemed distracted. Bruce Pavitt got up to speak, briefly and sadly. "A lot of what happened for [Sub Pop] happened in tandem with what happened for Nirvana. . . . We should remember and celebrate the positive things about Kurt Cobain."

Later, many of the party-goers headed on to Linda's

Tavern, the nearby bar partially owned by Sub Pop's Jonathan Poneman and Pavitt, where Kurt was apparently seen a week before he took his life.

Record stores were picked clean—by 3 P.M. Friday, there was scarcely a Nirvana record to be bought in Seattle. Many stores had even taken their phones off the hook—"we've not had a day like this since John Lennon!" sighed one of the handful still answering.

On both sides of the Atlantic, the following week's chart showed Nirvana's entire back catalog had made sizeable—if not utterly unpredictable—leaps up the chart. *In Utero* jumped from #72 to #27, with sales in excess of 40,000; *Nevermind* tripled the 7,000 copies it had sold the previous week, to climb from #167 to #56; *Incesticide* re-entered the chart at #147; sales of *Bleach* went from 2,000 in the week before Kurt's death, to 9,000. And that only included sales figures up to the Sunday following the tragedy.

Where Nirvana albums were exhausted, fans started picking up Hole's instead. *Live Through This*, the band's second album, was released on the Tuesday following Kurt's death, a date which had been scheduled some time before, and at least one Seattle record store was able to report, "we sold out the day we got it," Rich Price, store manager of the downtown branch of Musicland, told the *Post-Intelligencer*. "A lot of people have been requesting it. There's definitely a buzz going on. It was getting good reviews before [Kurt's] death, but [the death] has been a catalyst."

Yet amid so much activity, still there was little news to go on. Kurt's body was identified from his fingerprints, and by 7 P.M. Friday, the first black limousines were passing through the winding driveway to the house. The police had already abandoned the scene, to be replaced by a private security firm.

Courtney Love had yet to appear. News of her arrest the previous day had yet to surface, except as a very vague rumor which was promptly, and regrettably, dismissed even by hardened reporters. Instead, journalists and cameramen chased ghosts—one report insisted she had been sighted boarding a charter plane for Seattle at Van Nuys airport, another claimed she was in London, where Hole were scheduled to perform at the Astoria II the following Sunday.

As it transpired, she had flown to Seattle immediately upon hearing of her husband's death, booking a charter flight and making her way directly to Kurt's mother, Wendy O'Connor. "Every night I've been sleeping with his mother," she told the thousands of fans gathered for the memorial vigil that Sunday. "And I wake up in the morning and I think it's him, because her body's sort of the same."

She arrived at her now media-besieged home on Saturday. Michael Azerrad, author of Nirvana's *Come As You Are* biography, appeared at one point to deliver a message of thanks from Love to the assembled fans. Later, Courtney spoke briefly with MTV news reporter Tabitha Soren (who ironically was already in Seattle, filming a report on drug abuse). She read aloud several passages from Kurt's suicide note; the rest she reserved for the message she was tape recording for the following evening's memorial at the Seattle Center. She would read more in person at the family's own, private, service.

There, around two hundred friends and family, including the father Kurt had scarcely seen since his teens, his mother and sister Kim, his aunt Bev, and his paternal grandfather, Leland, gathered to pay their final respects. Dave Grohl and Chris Novoselic, Kim Deal and Peter Buck were there as well. Kurt's grandmother, Iris, wasn't; ill-health prevented her from making the journey up to Seattle. "Now I have no way to say goodbye," she reportedly told Aunt Bev.

After the service, a tape of some of Kurt's favorite music was played—Iggy Pop, the Beatles, Leadbelly and his own. Somehow, his inclusion within such esteemed company only seemed right.

At the same time, Courtney's tape recorded message was booming out over a now-silent Seattle Center. Other speakers—DJs, remembering their own encounters with Kurt, his step uncle, Larry Smith, recounting a few happy memories, the Reverend Towles, leading the crowd in a short but heartfelt prayer, had come and gone. Now Courtney was bathed in a spotlight she wished she had never, ever seen.

Her voice all but inaudible through her tears, Courtney began to read her late husband's last words. She'd prefaced them with a brave explanation—brave, because even in his last few moments, Kurt's thoughts were not only of his immediate family. They also went out to everybody who had ever bought a Nirvana record, everyone who had ever gone to see them play, everyone whose life would be touched, and somehow rendered a little bit sadder, by what he was about to do.

"I don't think it takes away from his dignity to read this, considering that it's addressed to most of you."

Later, there was some criticism within the media that so private a moment should be shared with 5,000-plus strangers, but Love was right to read it, just as she was right to appear personally at the memorial, shortly before it was over, traveling directly from Unity Church to sit quietly amidst the grieving fans.

She was right, too, to lead the crowd on tape into a chant of "asshole" in memory of her late husband. In the face of his own confession, that he took his life because he couldn't stand his job, it was the most honest response she could have delivered.

And today, most people agree with that.

But even as answers are finally given to the questions which have swirled round Seattle since the story first broke, as the cracked jigsaw puzzle of Kurt's last days is finally pieced together and solved, still there remain several pieces which might never be satisfactorily fit into place.

Why, when Cobain's delicate mental state was common knowledge, was he never pointed in the direction of help that he could trust?

Why, when his health was clearly endangering both his own well-being, and that of his band's, was more not done to discover what was wrong?

And why, before his body was even laid to rest, did one have the terrible feeling that he will not be the last pampered and sheltered superstar to die so adored and yet so alone? In a remark which is still being broadcast around the world, the first quotable quote from any grieving family member, Wendy O'Connor lamented that her son had finally joined "that stupid club," the club which is reserved for dead rock'n'rollers.

The news services gobbled her comment up greedily, even pausing to note that Kurt was 27 when he died, the same age as Jimi Hendrix and Jim Morrison. But Hendrix and Morrison, Sid Vicious, Brian Jones, Andrew Wood and the all other stars who shine in rock'n'roll heaven, didn't deliberately choose to die, didn't calmly write a letter to their families before placing a shotgun in their mouths and firing.

There was nothing accidental about Kurt Cobain's death, and no room for error either. Even without the suicide note, nobody could ever say it was another cry for help which went horribly, tragically, wrong. Cobain knew what he was doing, as certainly as he knew why he did it. And in making that decision, he made another, too. He wasn't joining some "stupid club" . . . or if he was, it wasn't the one which his mother had in mind.

Kurt Cobain doesn't belong with the Morrisons and Moons of this (or any other) world. He didn't die of rock'n'roll. Instead, remember him alongside the Joplins and the Shannons, the Garlands and Monroes. The superstars who died of neglect.

Acknowledgments

It's no secret that a biography such as this demands the time and attention of many more people than the author, and in this instance I am most heavily indebted to my wife, Jo-Ann, who worked at least as hard as I did in gathering and collating information, and without whom, I would never have been able to piece together the chronology of Kurt Cobain's last weeks on earth.

I would also like to thank Grant Alden, for graciously opening his own files to me; Jeff Ressner, John Aizlewood and Joe Banks, each of whom opened doors I might otherwise have walked straight by; Chris Nickson, Wendy Weisberg and Jeff Tamarkin, for gathering up so much more research material; Charles Cross, Gillian Gaar, Robert Roth, and especially, Amy Mueller for being a great friend. Snarleyyow, K-Mart, Geoff Monmouth and Anchorite Man also proved irreplaceable pillars of support, particularly as the deadline loomed closer. And finally, a special thank you to Tony Secunda and Jim Fitzgerald, for ironing out all the kinks (and pretty things).

My primary sources for the information contained in this book were my own interviews with many of the principal characers who appear herein: including Kurt Cobain, Dave Grohl and Chris Novoselic, of course, but

also Steve Albini, Buzz Osbourne, Dale Crover, and
Gina Birch.

In addition to these, Grant Alden kindly supplied me
with the transcripts of his own interviews with Jonathan
Poneman and Bruce Pavitt, Ben Shepherd, Chris and
Dave, and Buzz and Dale; while Jo-Ann Greene supplied her conversations with Chad Channing, Mark
Arm, Steve Turner, Daniel House and Nils Bernstein.
Grant and Jo-Ann also contributed greatly to my own
stockpile of interviews with people who, for various
reasons, declined to be identified in this book.

In addition to these sources, I also had access to
several hundred articles and news clippings, drawn from
several dozen different magazines. Of these, I would
particularly like to acknowledge *Alternative Press*, the
Seattle Times and *Post-Intelligencer* newspapers, *The Rocket*,
Q, *Select*, *Vox*, *Spin*, *Rolling Stone*, *Option*, the *Los Angeles
Times* and *Los Angeles Weekly*, *Details*, *Sounds*, *Melody Maker*
and the *New Musical Express*. Of special value were:
"Cobain Found a Kindred Spirit in Frances Farmer's
Tragic Life" by William Arnold [*Seattle Post-Intelligencer*
April 14, 1994]; "Aberdeen Betrays the Origins of the
World's Greatest Garage Band" by Patrica MacDonald
[*Seattle Times*, March 8, 1992]; "Nirvana: Inside the
Heart and Mind of Kurt Cobain" by Michael Azerrad
[*Rolling Stone*, April 16, 1992].

I would also like to acknowledge my debt to Michael
Azerrad's authorized biography of Nirvana, *Come As You
Are*, in particular, the chapter on Kurt Cobain's childhood and early teen years; in other respects, it served as
the starting point for a great many of my own inquiries.

Finally, I should point out that I have occasionally
taken the liberty of attempting to recreate passages of
dialogue between certain characters in this book. This
has been done only after thoroughly checking all the
available facts, to ensure that the resultant account of
events remains accurate.

Crisis Hotlines

If you or someone you know is in crisis or thinking about suicide, help is only a phone call away. Professional counselors are standing by and ready to speak with you for as long as you need about any and all of your problems. No judgment. No advice. No questions asked. Just talking and listening.

Don't suffer alone. Take the first step by asking for help.

All phone calls are free and confidential.

Mental Health Access Line	1-800-827-7571
Boy's Town National Hotline	1-800-448-3000
The "9" Line Covenant House	1-800-999-9999
National Teenline	1-800-522-8336